THE
BOB LOVE
STORY

If It's Gonna Be, It's Up to Me

Robert Earl Love with Mel Watkins

Foreword by Michael Jordan

CB

CONTEMPORARY BOOKS

Library of Congress Cataloging-in-Publication Data

Love, Robert Earl, 1942–
     The Bob Love story : if it's gonna be, it's up to me / Robert Earl Love with Mel Watkins.
          p.   cm.
     ISBN 0-8092-2597-2
     1. Love, Robert Earl, 1942–   2. Basketball players—United States—Biography.   3. Chicago Bulls (Basketball team)   I. Watkins, Mel, 1940–II. Title.
GV884.L64   A3   2000
796.357'092—dc21
[B]   99-46672

Interior design by Nick Panos

Published by Contemporary Books
A division of NTC/Contemporary Publishing Group, Inc.
4255 West Touhy Avenue, Lincolnwood (Chicago), Illinois 60712-1975 U.S.A.
Copyright © 2000 by Bob Love with Mel Watkins
All rights reserved. No part of this book may be reproduced, stored in a retrieval system, or transmitted in any form or by any means, electronic, mechanical, photocopying, recording, or otherwise, without the prior written permission of NTC/Contemporary Publishing Group, Inc.
Printed in the United States of America
International Standard Book Number: 0-8092-2597-2

00 01 02 03 04 05 LB 19 18 17 16 15 14 13 12 11 10 9 8 7 6 5 4 3 2 1

CONTENTS

FOREWORD

By Michael Jordan

Bob Love personifies the best qualities of an NBA player, both on and off the court. During his basketball career, he slashed his way through defensive players who marveled at his ability to score like few before or since. Often "Butterbeans," as he was known, led the Chicago Bulls in scoring.

I admired Bob's play because he was much more than a high scorer who dazzled his fans with sleight of hand moves that would leave him open for that pure jumper of his. He was also an outstanding defensive player.

When his basketball career ended, Bob Love found new challenges. Out of work and unable to overcome his childhood tendency to stutter, he faced an uncertain future. Fortunately, a speech therapist helped him overcome his speech difficulty. He joined the Chicago Bulls as Director of Community Relations. Speeches outlining his inspirational story have helped thousands of schoolchildren realize that nothing in life is impossible.

When the Chicago Bulls retired Bob Love's jersey, I joined cheering fans in applauding his lifetime of achievement in the game of basketball. I'm honored as a friend to write the foreword for his book, and I am certain that you are going to enjoy reading about one of the true legends of basketball.

PREFACE

By Stedman Graham

As we approach the beginning of the twenty-first century, the sports world has assumed the preeminent place in our popular culture once almost exclusively reserved for the Hollywood film industry and its larger-than-life movie stars. Superstar professional athletes, particularly basketball players, now command incomes, adulation, and worldwide renown that during Hollywood's heyday was reserved for such silver-screen legends as Clark Gable, Marilyn Monroe, or Sidney Poitier. Too often, however, the obsession with winning, the media's microscopic scrutiny and frenzied hype of sports events, and our own fascination with the extraordinary exploits and accomplishments of elite athletes obscure the less spectacular real-life battles that unfold beyond the playing field or arena. And, as *The Bob Love Story: If It's Gonna Be, It's Up to Me* vividly depicts, those personal, off-court struggles, which are often more challenging and threatening, usually demand as much strength and fortitude as the most dazzling athletic performance.

Robert Earl Love is presently the director of community relations for the Chicago Bulls; his number 10 jersey was retired (the second of only three players to be so honored) in 1994 and now hangs with the jerseys of Jerry Sloan and Michael Jordan in the United Center. His position as spokesman for the Bulls and his retired jersey are equally important to Bob "Butterbeans" Love. They represent triumphs achieved both off and on the basketball court over tremendous odds. And—like *Brian's*

Song (the moving story of an extraordinary friendship between football legend Gale Sayers and his teammate Brian Piccolo) and Arthur Ashe's memoir, *Days of Grace*—this inspiring account of Love's life transcends sports.

Despite the author's illustrious athletic career—a three-time All-American at Southern University in Baton Rouge, Louisiana, as well as the school's all-time leading scorer; a four-time NBA All-Star selection; and, until the arrival of Michael Jordan, record-holder in every offensive category for the Bulls—his remarkable memoir is a candid, intensely felt, human story that is primarily focused outside the sports arena. It is the inspirational tale of Love's roller coaster journey from abject poverty in rural Louisiana through stardom as a college and NBA basketball player; his devastating plummet to poverty, obscurity, and humiliating jobs as a dishwasher, busboy, and waiter after an injury forced his retirement from the NBA in 1977; and his fight to achieve a lifelong dream and overcome the speech impediment that had trapped him behind a wall of silence and plagued him throughout most of his life.

"The inability to communicate is a terrible thing," Robert Earl Love writes. But—plagued by a stuttering problem that limited his social life, restricted his earning power even as an NBA star, and, after he left basketball, nearly shattered his life—he refused to give up. "During my basketball career," he says, "I accomplished every goal that could be accomplished. I was All-American, All-Star, All-Pro, but, you know, I wasn't really satisfied. I cannot remember the first basket I made or the last basket I made. But since God has enabled me to speak, I can remember almost every speech I've made, nearly every face that I've seen in the audiences. I'm enjoying my life now much more than I did when I was in the NBA. And it's all because I didn't give up my dreams. *I refused to play the victim.*"

A wily old Ashanti proverb advises that "a man scratches where he can reach." And in *The Bob Love Story: If It's Gonna Be, It's Up to Me*, Butterbeans Love dramatically reaffirms that the breadth of our reach is largely controlled by our own courage and determination. His inspirational testament should be required reading for every youngster who mistakenly assumes that athletic achievement alone (even All-Pro status in the NBA) is an instant cure-all for life's personal challenges. In addition, the author's indomitable will and gutsy, positive outlook should encourage and inspire everyone to extend their reach, follow their dreams, and resolutely confront life's obstacles—whether they arise in the form of racial or sexual discrimination, poverty, or physical disabilities.

ACKNOWLEDGMENTS

WOULD LIKE TO THANK some of the people whose advice and assistance have guided and supported me through the years, making this book possible.

Foremost, I owe a special debt to my family—particularly my mother, Lula Bell Hunter Cleveland, and my grandmother, Ella Mae Hunter—whose dedication and love got me through the early years.

For helping me hone my athletic skills and become a responsible adult, I would also like to thank my high school football coach, William Washington (and his wife Dorothy); my high school basketball coach, Payne Montgomery; my college basketball coaches, Richard Mack (and his wife Arlen) and John Brown.

I also thank John, Bruce, and Jim Nordstrom for giving me an opportunity when no one else was willing to take a chance on me; Steve Schanwald and Jerry Reinsdorf for not only allowing me to return to the Chicago Bulls but also for their support and friendship, and Susan Hamilton, the world's best speech therapist, for helping me overcome my disability. Without her, I might still be trapped behind a wall of silence. I would also like to thank my literary agents Bob Williams of Burns Sports and Frank Weimann of The Literary Group for their determination on this project, as well as Ken Samelson and Blythe Smith at Contemporary Books.

Last, apologizing in advance for anyone I may overlook, I want to thank some of the many friends who have stepped up to help when I have been most in need, either materially or spiritually. They include: Eric Spitzer, Mike Webb, Jack Harbour, Mickey Norton, Gery Chico, Don Dobie, William H. Louis, Mark and George Wiegel, Jim and Eric Griggs, Tim Rand, Jerry Rich, Dr. Paul Vallas, Jerry Cochran, John Hyland, Chuck Walsh, John Sickage, Chuck Ceberhart, Neil Berge, Rick Petersen, Dave Chobar, Jerome Rowan, Dwan Brown, Bobby Wilson, Dave Kurland, Sara Salzman, Tony Rokita, Joe O'Neil, Kevin Riley, Stu Bookman, Irwin Mandel, Jerry Krause, Michele Cunningham, Claudia Randell, Sebrina Brewster, Larry Klein, Ronnie Sue Toth, John Kolvach, Larry Stonage, Nate Cain, Rine Hammer, Dan Lewis, Brad Wenner, Al Bartley, Aaron and Abe Regans, Barney and Carol Barnett, Charles Dudley, Paul Mitchell, Richard Frame, Mark Bogan, Dr. Jim Oliver, Mark Dym, Al Muller, Robert Butch Brest, Chris Townsen, Steve and John Nicholson, Kim Benolken, George McDade, John Celmer, Jane Lucas, Robert Hatcher, Theo, John Sikith, Dominick Desantis, Leslie "Buddy" Flemming, Tim Bradford, Jim Osborne, Richard T. Vollmer, Reverend Jesse L. Jackson, President John Stroger, Troy Ratliff, Betty Hancock Perry, Lisa Gamze, Kevin Coile, Dr. John West, James W. Jesk, Jack and Mark Childers, Mark Wojack, Delores Jordan, Oscar Robertson, Bill Russell, Jerry West, Jerry Jacova, and Mayor Richard M. Daley Jr.

INTRODUCTION

FROM AS EARLY AS I CAN REMEMBER, I always had these vivid dreams. They just shot into my mind and took hold. Funny, because after a while they seemed just as real as the outside world. And somehow, even before I was a teenager, I knew I'd make them come true.

At first, I used to dream about being a star football player. My grandmother had this little old radio, which was full of static and didn't pick up signals too clearly, but in the evenings I'd huddle around with her kids—my aunts and uncles—and listen to sports events. They would broadcast pro games from the NFL and some regional college games. There were a lot of great players, and I would sit there and imagine that I was in their shoes. I could see myself streaking down the field, catching a long pass, carrying the ball, cutting through the line, slipping tackles, and streaking toward the end zone, outrunning everybody in sight . . . or I'd take the ball from the center, drop back into the pocket, and throw a perfect spiral to one of my teammates.

I practiced throwing the football all day long, and at night I'd dream about it. When I wasn't playing in a game with my friends, I'd go out in the yard alone, roll up a newspaper or magazine, and pretend I was a quarterback. I'd imagine myself calling the signals and taking the snap; then I'd roll out to avoid the rush before I threw a bullet down the field. The great Baltimore quarterback Johnny Unitas was my hero. And, in my mind, like him I always made the big plays. In fact, I never failed to complete the game-winning pass as the clock ran down.

I didn't give up on my Johnny Unitas fantasies, but, as a teenager, I developed a serious interest in basketball. I started imagining myself out on the court with the best players. I listened to the games—heard the great North Carolina and Kentucky teams, the great Kansas team with Wilt Chamberlain, and the Ohio State and Cincinnati championship teams at night on that same little radio. During the play-offs, they sometimes broadcast NBA games and I'd hear about superstars like Ed Macauley, Bob Pettit, Elgin Baylor, Oscar Robertson, and Bill Russell. I dreamed that I was out on the court playing against those guys, and, in my mind, I actually heard the crowds cheering.

We couldn't afford a backboard and basket or a real ball, so at first I took a wire hanger from my grandfather's closet, shaped it like a hoop, and nailed it up on the side of the house. Then I found one of my grandfather's old discarded socks, filled it with paper and grass, and shaped it into a ball. It wouldn't bounce so I couldn't dribble it. But I took that little makeshift ball, which even after being beaten against the house or rolled in the dirt and mud, always smelled like Grandpa's feet, and I stayed out there shooting for hours.

That wire hoop was only about eight or nine feet off the ground, but I'd be out there juking and faking, soaring and dunking with that old sock as if I were in an NBA arena. At that time, of course, kids didn't want to be like Mike; they wanted to float like Elgin. He was an amazing ballplayer, and I tried to imitate all of his moves. In my head, I played against the best players alive right out there in my backyard. Not even Bill Russell, the greatest defensive player alive, could stop me. I never lost a game.

I realized later that my fascination with sports was in part a way of escaping everyday reality. From the time I was a little boy I had a severe speaking problem. In church, in the classroom, or trying to talk to the girls or hang out with the fellows, I was always being teased and embarrassed. It got so bad that sometimes I wouldn't say anything, wouldn't even answer a question, because I knew somebody would laugh at me. It was as if I was trapped behind a wall of silence. But on the football field or basketball court, at least in my dreams, no one teased me. The kids may have ridiculed me in class, but in my fantasies I was never the butt of anyone's joke. I was a hero, a superstar. Nobody laughed—no one cared about my stuttering.

I think that's why, even while I holed up in athletic fantasies, I had another recurring vision. During most of my childhood and all through the years when I played professional basketball in the NBA, I kept dreaming that one day I was going to become a great speaker. At first, I dreamed that I was a preacher, like Reverend I. J. Jordan, the minister at New Morning Star Baptist Church in Bastrop, Louisiana, where I grew up. And later I would dream that I was Dr. Martin Luther King Jr. or John F. Kennedy or one of those guys. I saw myself on a big stage, behind a podium, speaking to thousands of people. They were stretched out as far as you could see—like the rows of cotton we saw on those mornings when we went out to work on the Higginbottom plantation. And words would just flow out of my mouth, smooth as music. Sometimes the vision was so real I could actually see the smile on people's faces, hear them cheer. The sound of all the applause and screaming would echo in my ears until it was almost deafening.

1

BEGINNINGS ON THE BAYOU

There was always a feeling of joy and
warmth about that house.

I WAS BORN DECEMBER 8, 1942, on the O'Neill plantation in a little town called Delhi in Louisiana. My mother, Lula Bell Hunter, was only fifteen years old; and my father, Benjamin Edward Love, had been drafted earlier that year and was still in the army. They never got married, so my mother was still living with her parents. At the time, like a lot of black southern families, my mother's folks still worked and lived on a plantation. I was born in their house, the last member of my family to be born on a plantation.

Right after my birth, the owner of the plantation told my mother that she had to go back to work in the fields. But my grandmother, Ella Mae Hunter, wouldn't hear of it. She kept telling him that it was too soon for Lula Bell to return to work—no way she was going back to the cotton fields to chop and pick that quickly. They tell me Ella Mae got right in that man's face and refused to budge, something that very few black people did back then. Finally he got fed up and told my grandparents that if Lula Bell didn't work they had to get off the O'Neill plantation.

The next morning, my grandfather, William Hunter, was up at dawn. He got on his mule and rode off to a nearby town called Tallulah. A day later, he came back driving an old rickety wagon. It wasn't much, but he piled everything we had into that wagon: the dishes, beds, table, chairs, and mattresses. Then he loaded the whole family—me, Lula Bell, his wife, and their other twelve children—and we left. We rode that cramped, mule-drawn wagon all the way to Tallulah, and we stayed there for over a year.

Life in Bastrop

Later, we moved a little farther up north to a town called Bastrop, which was about fifteen miles away. It was a pretty good-size town, bigger than Delhi or Tallulah, with a population of about 8,000. The downtown business district ran about six blocks in each direction, and there were a couple of fair restaurants, a diner, and some nice stores. It had two picture shows, the Rose Theater and the Swan Theater. Of course, both of them were segregated; we had to sit upstairs, and the white folks sat downstairs. You bought a ticket, and when you went inside there was a guy who ushered blacks to the right and whites to the left. Unlike Delhi, Bastrop had its own courthouse and firehouse, as well as a jailhouse, which was near the railroad tracks. There was also a black section of town, which had a store, a few little restaurants, and some juke joints and clubs. Those clubs were all in the area we called the Block, and on weekends it was jumping. Black folks from the surrounding towns would stream in to party. Bastrop wasn't that big but it was kind of a hub for blacks in that section of Louisiana.

There was also a big mill, which employed a few hundred people. The Bastrop Paper Mill made boxes, packages, napkins, all kinds of paper products, and distributed them throughout Louisiana and Arkansas. If you were up early in the morning, you would see these guys driving big old log trucks, hauling pine trees maybe 100 feet long on the back. They were on their way to the mill's treatment plant, where the logs were converted into paper. And every afternoon you could smell the stench from the plant all over town.

It was strongest in our neighborhood because the mill had built what they called a pulp ditch that ran right through the middle of the black section of town before it emptied into the

2

Bayou Bartholomew, a marshy lake at the edge of town. That ditch was less than a mile from my grandmother's house. And every day the by-products and chemical waste from the plant were dumped into that open ditch. Some days it almost made you gag—it smelled like rotten eggs. Bastrop had some other drawbacks, but I think that smell was the worst. It was horrible, and I had to put up with it for eighteen years—except for the time I spent in college at Southern University, where I lived until I left the South and started playing pro basketball.

When we moved to Bastrop, my grandparents got a mortgage for a small place on Henry Street. It was a wooden two-bedroom railroad- or shotgun-style house with a tin roof. It had a bedroom on each end, and the kitchen was in the middle. There was no indoor plumbing, so everyone had to use the outhouse and bathe in a big old tub. We didn't have electricity until after I started high school, so during my childhood we had kerosene lamps in every room. That's the way it was in southern country towns back then, but we didn't mind too much. You just accepted what you had and made do.

Of course, some things bothered me more than others. I never got used to using that outhouse, for instance. Living in the country can be very scary for a child, and nothing frightened me more than going to the outhouse at night. It was usually pitch dark out there, and I'd be dodging mosquitoes and stepping on frogs and worms and what have you. I could hear snakes and other animals crawling around in the bushes. As a little kid, I was always worried about falling into that toilet. Going out there scared me to death.

The rest wasn't all that rough. We didn't have a refrigerator, but every morning the ice man would come by and bring twenty-five pounds of ice. My grandfather would put it in the bottom of the icebox, and although it was messy sometimes, it kept everything cool all day long. And on hot days, that old tin roof made it seem like a furnace inside the house. But when it rained at night, I would just lie in bed and listen to the sound of rain beating down on the roof. It was like music to my ears.

I still don't know how all thirteen children slept in that back bedroom. There were only two beds, and each night everybody would scramble to see who could get a spot. Some of us ended up on a bed, and the others slept on one of the pallets my grandmother made by stuffing cotton into hand-sewn quilts. We had potbelly stoves in the bedrooms and kitchen, and on cold nights everybody would huddle up together to try to keep warm. It wasn't always easy, but we had fun. There was always a feeling of joy and warmth about that house. Nowadays, when I mention how crowded it was, people think about it and start shaking their heads, but it wasn't all that bad for us. It was all we knew, and we made the best of it.

Mom, Dad, and Baba

The first few years in Bastrop, I lived with my grandparents; they and my aunt Nancy raised me during that time. See, when I was a little over a year old, my mother left Louisiana and went to Detroit. She stayed up north for over two years, trying to get herself together and, according to Ella Mae, raise money to send for me.

While she was away, my father was discharged from the army. He stopped by my grandparents' house to see me when he came through Bastrop to see his own folks. I don't remember much about it, but years later my grandmother told me that when he arrived he set me down on his knee, pulled out his wallet, and flashed a thick wad of bills. He had all the cash he'd saved while he was in the service. He told me to reach in the wallet and take whatever I wanted. My grandmother said she almost fainted when all I took was one dollar bill. "Took all my willpower to keep from reaching in there and helping you get what you deserved. Lord knows we coulda used it," she told me later. A few days afterward, Benjamin Love left town. I didn't see him again until I was thirty-three years old.

Then a year or so later, my mother returned to Bastrop. Things hadn't worked out for her in Detroit. By that time, Lee Cleveland, one of her old boyfriends who had also been drafted, had returned and settled down near Bastrop. They went out together for about a year, before Baba—that's what everybody called Lee—married my mother.

From the beginning, he made it clear that he didn't want me around. But my mother insisted that I stay with them, and although I still spent a lot of time at my grandparents' house, I moved into their house on Jackson Street. It was awkward even before they had their own kids. I remember my stepfather always having his face twisted up in this mean scowl whenever he stared down at me. He was a heavyset, intimidating, dark-skinned man who always looked like he was mad at something or somebody. Most of the time, it seemed to be me.

In part, it stemmed from an old rivalry with my father. When she was a teenager, my mother was about the most beautiful girl in Delhi, Louisiana. Brown-skinned and about 5 feet 6 inches tall, she was being chased and hit on by nearly every young boy in the area. My father and Baba had been big rivals. Both of them tried to court her when they were in school. It turned out that my father beat his time. Before long, Benjamin Love and Lula Bell were going together. They never married, but when he left for the army that spring she was pregnant. I guess Lee never got over being outdone by my father. For him, I was a living reminder of his losing out.

There wasn't much I could do right around their house. Baba found fault with everything—stayed on my case. The smallest little mistake, like spilling some water or breaking a dish, resulted in a scolding or a beating.

I'm not sure how it began, but by the time I was four I had also started stuttering. One of my favorite uncles, Will, was a stutterer, and we all loved him. I think that part of my speech problem was that I really looked up to him. He was about twelve years older than I was, but when I was a kid we spent a lot of time playing together. I wanted to talk like Will, and early on, nobody stopped me. Anyway, when they finally noticed that it wasn't going away, most everyone tried to help me overcome the problem. My grandmother and mother were the most supportive. They'd tell me, "Don't worry, son. It's all

5

right," or encourage me with, "C'mon, Robert Earl, you can do it . . . spit it out." But Baba just looked at me and laughed, or shook his head like I was crazy or stupid.

When I was a kid, that man frightened me so much I'd start trembling the moment he walked through the door.

From the outside, their house looked exactly like my grandparents' place, which was a half mile away. But there was a big difference: it had electricity and an indoor toilet. At first, I think I appreciated that toilet more than anything else—I was still afraid of the outhouse. But I quickly discovered that going to the bathroom at my mother's house was sometimes just as scary. It was next to her bedroom, and most every time I got up to go to the bathroom at night I'd bump into something or make some noise. Even flushing the toilet disturbed her and my stepfather. He would wake up furious. "What the hell's wrong with you, boy! Don't you know I got to work tomorrow?" he'd yell. "Get back in that bed and be quiet!"

Sometimes he'd get up, storm out to the bathroom, and just slap me. It got so bad I was afraid to go to the toilet, so I'd just lie there and try to hold it in; it was during that time that I began wetting the bed. I was ashamed to stay there in my bed but too scared to get up. I didn't get over that fear until I left my stepfather's house for good.

A little over a year after they were married, their first son, Lee Jr., was born. After that, things got even worse. With his own child in the house, my stepfather seemed even more resentful of me. His son treated me like a brother, and we got along fine. But Baba made it clear that I wasn't really part of their family. To him, I was just an intruder. On holidays or his birthday, for instance, Lee would get all kinds of presents; I was lucky if I got anything. I'd sit there and open my one little gift on Christmas—usually something small like a coloring book that my mother or grandmother had bought—and watch as Lee unwrapped things like trucks and building blocks and cowboy pistols. All I could do was hope he would let me play with his toys. I could see that my mother was upset by it, but I guess she was afraid to speak up. She never said a word. It hurt, but I was happy to get the old toys when Lee got tired of playing with them. I just tried to keep quiet and stay out of my stepfather's way.

I found that the easiest way to do that was to spend more time at my grandparents' house, and fortunately Ella Mae encouraged it. I'd walk over there during the day and just hang around. I knew that once it got dark she wouldn't let me go back to Baba's house by myself. And despite my fear of the outhouse, I was a much happier child when I stayed with my grandparents. Their children were like brothers and sisters to me, and Ella Mae and William treated me more like a son than my stepfather.

My Grandfather

My grandfather, who was part Cherokee Indian, had this reddish complexion and hair like corn silk. He had married my grandmother when she was fifteen and he was in his forties. Back in those days age differences really didn't matter. Once the parents gave the OK, you could marry anybody you chose, and nobody made a fuss about it. When I was a child, he was already in his eighties, but he was still a cheerful, good-looking man. He always had a smile and a positive word for everybody. He kept us all laughing.

He was retired, and every month he'd get a Social Security check for about sixty dollars. I don't know how, but except for a little money that Grandma made doing odd jobs, they paid the bills and supported all their kids on that check.

Their mail was delivered to a post office box, and sometimes I'd go with them when they picked it up. The first thing they did was go to the liquor store and cash the check. He didn't write too well, so Grandma helped him scribble his name on the back. She always gave Grandpa two dollars to put in his pocket. And before they left, she would buy him a pint of Old Crow bour-

7

bon. He kept that bottle of whiskey in his coat pocket at all times, and usually it would last him nearly until his next check arrived.

But before we went home, Grandma would go to the grocery store. She would buy oil, cornmeal, a large box of powdered milk, a big sack of flour, lima beans (which we called butter-beans), stuff like that. And she always bought a case of chicken backs and chicken feet. There wasn't much meat on them, but we had chicken nearly every day at my grandparents' house. On the way home, she would stop and buy more food from our neighbors. A lot of families had gardens, and they sold fruit and vegetables to other folks—things like greens and cabbage and watermelons. We also went fishing down at the bayou that ran around the edge of the city. Grandpa and I caught perch, cat-fish, or sometimes a few crappie or bass. A lot of times you could just stand there, throw the hook in, and catch a fish—sometimes two or three.

We struggled, but there was always a way to get enough food. And even after Grandma paid maybe three or four dol-lars for the bills, she was able to keep a little money in her pocket to help us get by during the rest of the month.

When we got back home, Grandpa would sit out on the porch, unscrew the top on his bottle, pour himself a capful, and drink it down straight. He never poured it in a glass. At his age, Grandpa wasn't too active. It seemed like he was always out there on the porch. He would wake up, have breakfast, then go out and take his favorite seat. A lot of times I'd come home from school and he would have his chin resting on his cane. He always had a little comb in his pocket. I'd take his comb and scratch his head or comb his hair for maybe an hour or so. He would rest on his cane and go to sleep.

He had a friend who lived across the street, and when he came over to visit Grandpa would give him a little cap of whis-key. They called it a pick-me-up. And most days they would sit out there joking, laughing, and lying all afternoon. Sometimes after Grandpa took a sip of whiskey and smacked his lips, he would lean back in his chair and start philosophizing.

"Robert Earl, I'm gonna tell you the secret to a long life," he told me one time. "If you want to live long and stay healthy, go to the bathroom when you get up every morning, take one shot of whiskey every day, and don't mess with no old women." He'd pause before he looked up, laughed, and winked. "Old women give you worms, son."

Of course, he never said that in front of my grandmother.

Grandpa had a hundred sayings like that, and most times he'd crack up any adults who listened. I loved him, and I'd sit there and listen even though I didn't always know what he was talking about. He was something else. By the time I reached my teens, my grandmother refused to sleep with him because she didn't want any more kids. He had fourteen children by her and eight more by his first wife. I was in college when he died in 1963. He was over 100 years old, and he was still walking around until the day he got sick and they took him to the hospital. That night, he just went to sleep and never woke up.

My Grandmother

Still, no one had as much of an impact on my childhood as my grandmother. Ella Mae was a strong, imposing dark-skinned woman with big, sparkling eyes. She was about 5 feet 10 inches, maybe a little taller, and had an overwhelming presence, physically and otherwise. She was the kind of person you didn't want to cross, especially if it concerned her children or family. I'll never forget what she did to this kid named Bullrow who lived right down the street from us. Bullrow was one of the neighborhood bullies, and he was always beating up on my uncle Will and teasing him about his stuttering.

One afternoon Will and one of my aunts got into an argument with Bullrow. I don't know what it was about, but Bullrow punched my uncle, then jumped on top of him and started choking him. The fight started right down the street from my grandmother's house, and she saw what was happening. I was inside the house when she rushed outside and started yelling,

9

"Bullrow! Bullrow, you better turn my son loose. Don't you choke my boy."

I don't know if he heard her or not, but he didn't let go of Will. That's when my grandmother picked up a stick, ran out to the street, and whacked Bullrow across his back and head. It wasn't a big stick, so it couldn't have hurt that much, but it nearly scared him to death. He jumped up screaming and ran off down the street.

Later that evening, Bullrow's daddy, Buddy Brown, came by and knocked on my grandmother's door. He was a short, stocky fellow, but he didn't intimidate Grandma in the least. She came to the door and said, "What you want, Buddy?"

"I heard that you hit my boy," Buddy said. "He said you hit him in the back and ran him off with a stick." He was standing out in the yard like he was going to do something, but my grandmother didn't even hesitate. She picked up the ax handle she kept by the door and stepped outside. Got right in his face. "Yeah, that's right," she said, "and I'm gonna hit you upside your head if you don't get out of my yard."

Buddy took a few steps back when my grandmother started waving the ax handle, and I came out of the house right behind her. I was only about six years old then, but I was going to help her if I could. Buddy could see my grandmother wasn't kidding. He knew that it wasn't the time to be messing with her. "All right, Miz Hunter," he said. "We'll straighten this out later on." He turned around and stormed out of the yard.

My grandmother didn't take no mess. She was one fierce woman. And over the years, I grew closer to her and learned more from her than from anyone I met. Whenever I struggled or faced some serious challenge, I tried to imagine how she might react.

2

EARLY CHILDHOOD MEMORIES

*We had a very tight-knit household, and most
of my fondest childhood memories revolve
around the things we did together at home.*

BEFORE I STARTED ELEMENTARY SCHOOL, my family and
friends hadn't paid much attention to my stuttering, and it
didn't seem to be a big problem for me. But that all changed
when I began first grade at the local Catholic school, Our Lady
Help of Christian, which we all called OLHC. For me, it was a
disaster.

The school was on West Madison, about four miles from my
grandmother's house. And since my aunt Minnie Merle, who
was only a year older than I was, had also started there, we
walked to school together almost every morning.

They had very tight rules about everything. We had to wear
identical uniforms—brown pants and white shirts—and everybody had to attend church each morning before school started.
The nuns who taught us were strict disciplinarians. For one
thing, they required that the students have their own notebooks,
pencils, and other supplies. Now, neither my parents nor my
grandparents had enough money to afford that stuff. So most
of the time Minnie and I would show up in class without a pen-
cil, notebook, coloring book, or some other item that was
needed. We had to scramble around trying to borrow them.
The worst thing was that the nuns didn't have any patience
with my speech problem, and whenever I couldn't answer a
question quickly enough, they would march over and slap me
across the knuckles with a ruler. I was one bruised child after

a week in that school; luckily my mother got me out of there. I went to the Catholic school for three months. When my mother found out what was going on, she had me transferred to Morehouse Parish Training School, which was on the same street but a little closer to my house. The next year Minnie Merle also transferred.

Unlike the Catholic school, my teachers at Morehouse were black; they were also much more lenient and sympathetic to my speech problem. That was particularly true of Mrs. Mozelle Moore, my first grade teacher. I'm not sure if she'd had any previous experience with kids who had speech problems, but she knew more about stuttering than anyone else I'd met. She treated it as a serious disability and helped guide me through my second year of school. In fact, she took me under her wing and watched out for me throughout the next two years—stopping in my classes to make sure I was doing OK, even though she wasn't my teacher. I was in the fourth grade when we heard that she had died, and that evening I went home and cried. She was a caring, dedicated teacher, and I missed her guidance.

Overall though, at the elementary school and later at Morehouse Parish High School, which was right next door, most of the teachers were very good about helping me—giving me more credit for my test scores and the papers I wrote than for class participation. Most times when they saw me sliding down in my seat or ducking behind the kid in front of me during classroom recitation, they didn't call on me. They would usually assume I was embarrassed or too nervous and pass me by. In fact, some of them were too good about it. Sometimes teachers would tell me, "Don't worry, Robert, take your time." I appreciated their concern, but I still had to laugh to myself. Hell, if I'd taken my time, I might still be up there trying to talk.

Facing the Laughter

The teachers were fine; it was the other students who often made it rough for me. Kids are going to be kids, and just as at most other elementary schools, there was a lot of wisecracking and teasing at Morehouse. It just so happened that because of my speech problem, I was usually the butt of the joke. Now, most of the time it was just good-natured ragging among friends—you know, "Damn, Bob, we ain' got all day—you got to let us know before tomorrow, my man." And, of course, I'd hear those "easy for you to say" jokes over and over. Still, when my boys were around, I tried laughing right along with everybody else.

But sometimes it got vicious. When I was in the third grade, for instance, the school bully, Peter, used to pick on me every day. He was a big, heavy kid who was a couple of grades ahead of me, and he used to terrorize everybody. He was one of those guys who didn't care how he looked. Seemed like he never combed his hair or brushed his teeth or washed. He was nasty, one of those ashy kids who had that white stuff in the corner of his mouth. Whenever I saw him coming, I knew it meant trouble. He'd laugh and say, "Uh-uh, uh, Rrr . . . Rrrr . . . Robert, what we goin' do today?" Then he'd either punch me or jump on my back and make me ride him part of the way home from school. It wasn't just me—he picked on nearly all the younger kids. He dropped out of school just after I reached the fifth grade, and everybody was happy then.

Peter was an exception; but some of the other kids could be just as hurtful without even knowing it. They'd snicker and laugh every time I tried to join in and say something. I was always ashamed, always trying to sidestep speaking unless I had to, but I didn't want to just give up, avoid people, and withdraw into my own little shell. So I tried to fight it; I struggled to speak as well as I could.

That's not to say that there weren't times when it nearly got the best of me. Morehouse was only a couple of miles away from my grandmother's house, and some days, after I'd passed the New Morning Star Baptist Church and J. D.'s Grocery Store and got close to school, my stomach would be in knots. I'd panic. My heart would start pounding and I'd get so scared that I could hardly breathe; it's a wonder I didn't have a heart

13

attack. I wanted to turn around and go home, especially on those days when I knew I'd have to make some presentation or recite something in front of my class. See, whenever I stood up to speak, I knew that nearly everybody in the class would bust out laughing. Still, I usually bit my lip and just went ahead and faced it.

Good Friends and Good Times

Minnie Merle, my grandmother's youngest kid, would always encourage me and try to help me through the rough times at school. She was really my closest friend when I was growing up. We went to school together, played together, and hung out with each other. We also got into a lot of trouble together. She was my aunt, but she was also my best pal, and we looked out for each other.

I remember once when she got into an argument with a kid named Bubba Red, who lived across the street. It got out of hand, and Bubba hit Minnie with a stick. When she told me about it, I told her I was going to get him for her. So Minnie Merle invited Bubba over to the house one day, and while he was out in the yard I got a hammer and cracked him upside the head. That was one of the times we got into trouble. When my grandmother found out about it, she tore up both of our behinds.

As a young kid, before I got to maybe the sixth grade, I really didn't have a lot of close friends outside of Minnie and my family. I enjoyed doing things by myself; I guess I was always kind of a loner. I was also a little shy around the girls because of my speech problem. I worried about embarrassing myself. Of course, that didn't mean that I wasn't interested in them. We had a lot of pretty girls at my school, and since the high school was right next to it, we were always checking out the older girls. Some guys my age were out there sniffing around, trying to talk themselves into something, but it was some time before I worked up enough nerve to do anything except look.

I had problems talking to the girls, but I got along with everybody. Most of us walked to school every day, and we usually met up somewhere along the way. I'd always join the other kids, and we did what most kids do—throw rocks, pull the girls' ponytails, or maybe buss them with a few love licks. I was pretty good looking, and the girls always wanted to talk to me. They were friends, even though I didn't say much. Instead of trying to talk and joke with them, I got attention by showing off my athletic skills.

There was no swimming pool for blacks in Bastrop, but sometimes a bunch of guys would get together to go swimming down at the bayou. We would take off our clothes, tie a rope to a tree limb, swing out over the water, and dive in. Swimming naked was probably against the law, but nobody bothered us. We did have to watch out for snakes, though, and a couple of kids got tangled up in the undergrowth and drowned. It was dangerous, but at that age nobody seemed to mind. We always enjoyed ourselves.

When I was about eleven or twelve years old, I started going to the picture show with a group of guys. My favorite was the Swan Theater, which always showed cowboy movies on Sundays. We'd see Red Rider and Little Beaver, Roy Rogers, Zorro, or Lash LaRue. I loved those westerns. And on Saturdays they had a midnight show. Usually they featured some scary movie like Frankenstein or the Wolf Man. At around ten o'clock, we'd all get together and walk into town. We had to be careful because we walked right through this white neighborhood.

Black kids going through that neighborhood at night couldn't make any noise, so we had to be real quiet. We couldn't even walk on the sidewalk—we had to walk out in the street, on the blacktop. And we had to keep moving—we couldn't stop. If we did, they would call the police, and that was trouble. That's the way it was in the South during the early 1950s, but kids didn't get mad about it. In a way, it was like a challenge, a game. We pretended we were sneaking through enemy territory in one of those war movies.

The picture show was usually over at about one thirty. And

by the time we left the movie, everybody was scared. When we got a few blocks away from the movie, there were no street lights. It was pitch dark outside. At that hour, we couldn't go back through the white neighborhood, so we had to take the long route back. That meant going through the black section of town, with the bars and after-hours joints, then walking through St. John's Cemetery, the town's black graveyard. All of us had heard ghost stories from the old folks, so whenever a bush shook or the moon disappeared behind a cloud and the shadows changed, we imagined that it was Dracula or Frankenstein or the Wolf Man and ran like hell. None of us really wanted to walk through that graveyard, but we didn't want to admit that we were scared, either. It was fun, but when I got home I was always shaking like a leaf.

I also played with the kids who lived across the street from us. They had a fairly big family with a half dozen kids, and a few of them were about my age. I went over to visit them sometimes and we played football and baseball together down at the neighborhood playground. But they were more interested in music and art than sports. I believe a few of them graduated from college and went into the music business. Except for pickup games at the playground, I didn't really get to know them well.

The one guy I spent a lot of time with was James Daniels. We called him Bullet. We hung out together, played ball and whatnot, and until he left Bastrop in the tenth grade, we were very good friends. We met in the seventh grade after he came from Arkansas to live with his mother, who was a schoolteacher. When she died a couple of years later, he had to move back to Arkansas to live with his father. I lost track of him after that. But while he was in town, we played on the junior high school football team together. We were quarterbacks, but I beat him out for the first team.

Years later, after I stopped playing for the Bulls, I ran into him in Chicago. He was a taxi driver. Then, after I moved to Seattle, I heard he'd been shot and killed when someone robbed his cab. When I heard that, I realized how lucky I had been. He was a good athlete and could easily have played college ball. But, like so many of the other guys I knew, he didn't want to go to college and nobody really pushed him to. Bullet just wasn't interested.

Weekends at Grandma's

Outside of my schoolmates and Bullet, I spent most of my time at home with my family and hung around my grandmother's house. Her number-one priority was raising her children in a Christian environment and keeping the family together. She went to church every Sunday, and she made sure that all of us went with her. We had a very tight-knit household, and most of my fondest childhood memories revolve around the things we did together at home.

The weekends were always special. On Saturday evenings, everybody had to take a bath. We started early because there were so many of us, and it wasn't that easy. We had to walk about a hundred yards to get water from the well, and by the time we got back with the bucket half the water had spilled out. Then we heated pots of water on the stove and poured them into a big old number-three tub. When we were little, there was always a lot of splashing and playing around, and Grandma would let us play if we didn't spend too much time in the tub. Somehow, before the night was over, everybody got a bath.

We got up early Sunday morning, and Grandma would make breakfast—homemade biscuits with fried-chicken gravy or syrup. We couldn't afford to buy the regular Brer Rabbit syrup all the time, so when we ran out of store-bought syrup, Grandma would make what we called sugar syrup. She would boil water in a pan, then put a half cup of sugar in there and cook it until it started bubbling. It wasn't as good as the store-bought syrup, but we loved it. We usually had some grits to go along with the biscuits. Most of the time that's all there was. It was a real treat when Grandma was able to fry a few chicken wings or maybe a little salt pork or fat back, which we called "streak-of-lean, streak-of-fat" because there was only a little band of lean meat in the middle of all that fat, and you seldom got any of the good part.

After breakfast, we'd run around trying to get dressed for church. Everybody would have to press his or her own clothes, and since we didn't have an electric iron we heated up a smoothing iron on the stove. When I was small, I wore these hand-me-down short pants and a white shirt. I don't think I had any dress clothes that fit before I got to junior high school. When everybody was ready, the whole family would walk down to the New Morning Star Baptist Church.

I went to Sunday school first, then I had to stay for morning services. Reverend I. J. Jordan would preach until one o'clock in the afternoon. Afterward, we all went back home and my grandmother would finish cooking Sunday dinner. That was the best meal we had all week, and everybody looked forward to it.

Sometimes Grandma would invite Reverend Jordan over for dinner. And, as much as I liked our preacher, that used to really upset me. See, the kids always had to wait until Grandma, the reverend, and the reverend's wife finished their meal before we could eat. It was an honor to have him at your house and all the church members offered him the best food they had. Whenever he was invited, my grandmother would go out and buy extra food—most of the time it was a whole chicken, with the breasts and thighs, the parts we seldom saw. She'd prepare a meal with the usual greens, potato salad, butterbeans, cornbread, and lemonade, but she added the best of the chicken for the preacher. And we had to wait and watch while he sat there and ate most of the good stuff. When he finished, he would lean back and say, "Sister Hunter, that sure was some good food."

Before he left, my grandmother would bring out the peach cobbler. The preacher would sit there and eat until he couldn't eat no more. By the time he and his wife finished, we were starving. And as soon as they got up, I would lead the rush to the table.

We got the leftovers—the chicken wings, necks, gizzards, and feet. Chicken feet were cheap, and since we didn't have a lot of money, my grandmother would buy them in big boxes. After cleaning them, she would dip them in a little flour and fry them. She served them with gravy. Nobody would think of eating them today; in fact, I don't even think they sell them anymore (somebody told me that they make gunpowder out of them). They probably had no nutritional value, but when they were prepared right, they were crunchy and good. Maybe I just didn't know any better, but I loved the way Grandma made them.

Just about the time we finished eating, around four o'clock, it was time to start getting dressed to go back to church. All the kids had to go to Baptist youth meeting, where we had Bible readings. After that, at about six o'clock, the older church members returned. They would always wear their Sunday best clothes, pressed suits and neat starched and ironed dresses. All the women on the church Mothers' Board had to wear white dresses and white bands around their heads. They were all older ladies, mostly grandmothers; along with the deacons, they were the most respected people in the congregation. My grandmother was on the Mothers' Board, and she sat with the others in a special section up near the front of the church.

The services started at about seven thirty. And once the preacher started, it seemed like he didn't want anybody to go home. Reverend Jordan would always stay up there until ten o'clock at night. He wouldn't stop until he got the whole church shouting; the sisters would be throwing their purses and jumping up and down. Some kids would get tired and start to doze off, but then one of the sisters would jump up and start hollering. Somebody would hit you upside the head or step on your foot, and you'd jump up scared to death. Nearly all the kids in my neighborhood went to church on Sundays, and nobody left before the services were over—no matter how much we might have wanted to be somewhere else. I still think that was why so

19

few of us got into trouble. The ones who got into trouble were the ones who didn't go to church—and nearly everybody went to church.

Grandma's Medicine

I had a lot of guidance and support from my grandparents and their kids when I was growing up, and despite the poverty I enjoyed myself. Still, by the time I reached the third grade, my stuttering was getting worse. Grandma always tried to help. I think she realized that one reason I spent so much time playing by myself out in our yard was that sometimes I felt isolated and different. But while Grandma encouraged me to dream, she didn't want me to get lost in a never-never land where I tried to escape the real world and the everyday problems I had to face. I think they call it "tough love" now, but even then she always made that plain as day.

A lot of times, after I'd been outside playing and had gotten real thirsty, I'd run into the kitchen and ask her to give me a glass of water. I was still stuttering badly, of course, so it took some time. And early on, she would stop washing dishes or whatever she was doing and just reach down, pat me on the back, and encourage me: "C'mon, Robert Earl, spit it out now, son." After a while though, whenever I ran in there and started tripping over my words, she'd say the same thing, but instead of patting me on the back she'd take the dishrag and pop me upside my head with it. It didn't help me "spit it out" any quicker, but I learned to stop asking and get that water for myself, real quick.

Grandma also prided herself on her remedies. One Sunday, when she took me to church, she stopped outside, reached into her purse, and pulled out a sack of marbles. She gave me three of them and told me to stick them under my tongue when I got up to recite in Sunday school class. When the teacher called me, I stood up, stuck the marbles in my mouth, and started trying to read. Before I even finished a sentence, I swallowed one. And for the next few weeks, I stood up there stammering and stuttering and swallowing one or two of those suckers. Finally I got tired of it. So one Sunday morning I said, "Grandma, I'm up to my neck in marbles and I'm still stuttering. Can we try something else?" She laughed and said OK. That was the last time I ever put a marble in my mouth.

Grandma wasn't the only one; lots of people suggested remedies for my speech problem when I was a kid—everything from holding my breath for a minute before I started to speak to pinching my fingers while I was talking. Nothing worked, and the problem didn't go away.

The Last Straw with Baba

Neither did the problems I had with my stepfather when I stayed at my mother's house. In fact, when I was about nine years old, that situation came to a head. I had always gotten along well with my half brother Lee, and although his father treated him much better than me, he never had an attitude toward me. Still, like most young kids, we had our little arguments and fights. One day when we were out playing in the woods with the new BB gun that his dad had given him, he got mad at me. He said, "Do you believe I'd shoot you?" I didn't think he would, so I said no.

I don't know what got into him that day, but he raised the gun and fired. I ducked and the BB grazed my nose. Although I wasn't seriously injured, it hurt like the devil. I was standing there holding my nose and trying to hold back my tears; then, when I saw him laughing, I got mad. I ran over and grabbed the gun. He started yelling and took off running, but I shot at him anyway. The BB hit him right upside the back of his head and bounced off. He didn't even pause, just grabbed at the back of his head and kept trucking.

I knew all hell was going to break loose when he got home and told his dad, but I followed him and stood outside. I was scared to go in there and face my stepfather. A few minutes

21

after I got there, Baba came busting through the door. He was so mad it looked like his eyes would pop out of his head. I turned tail and tried to run, but he was on me before I took a second step. He grabbed me by the neck, yanked his belt off, rolled it up, and starting whacking me with it. After a minute or two, my mother ran outside screaming and begged him to stop, but he held me down on the porch and kept beating me with the buckle of his belt. I was crying and yelling as loudly as I could. I actually thought I was going to die that evening. Finally, I managed to squirm away and break free. I ran directly to my grandmother's house. When she saw me coming through her gate with cuts and gashes all over my body, she almost fainted. My arms and legs were bleeding and my face was swollen and badly bruised; she couldn't believe it.

"Who did this to you, Robert Earl?" she screamed.

When I told her it was my stepfather, she didn't say a word, but I could tell that she was seething. That night, she just washed the blood off me, put me to bed, and went out to sit on the porch in her rocking chair.

The next afternoon, when he got off from work, my step-father came by her house to get me. My grandmother saw him coming and stood right inside the door, waiting to meet him. She always kept an ax handle there by the door, and when he stepped on the porch, she picked it up.

"I come to get Robert Earl," he said.

Now, normally my grandmother didn't curse. But that day she walked out to the fence holding that ax handle and stopped Baba before he entered the yard. "Get away from here you black motherfucker!" she shouted. "Don't you ever bring your ass to my house again."

My stepfather was shocked. I guess he didn't expect my grandmother to be so mad. Finally he just backed away, mumbling like *he* had a speech impediment. I went to visit my mother and sometimes saw Baba after that, but I lived with my grandparents until I finished high school and left Bastrop.

It wasn't until I was an adult that I learned that I probably got away from my stepfather's house just in time. That's when my aunts, Honey and Inez, told me about something that had happened a few years before the BB incident. Apparently, one day when my mother was out working, Honey had been looking after Lee Jr. when my stepfather came home early from work. She said he drew her aside, pointed to a butcher knife, and tried to convince her to cut my throat when I came home. She was shocked by the suggestion and, of course, refused. Still, for a long time she was too afraid to say anything to anyone. Later she told my grandmother, so Ella Mae had known how he felt about me for some time.

It turned out that I was the only one who didn't know how much my stepfather really resented my father's affair with Lula Bell. He was so dead set on destroying my father's memory that he was willing to destroy me. Despite everything else, I had to count myself lucky to get away from Baba with just a beating.

3

ANXIOUS ADOLESCENCE

*"The thing is, you gotta have a dream, son.
You gotta have a dream and you got to keep
it. You got to hold on to your dream. No
matter how bad things may look."*

AFTER MOVING OUT OF my stepfather's house for good, I spent even more time with my grandmother and my aunt Minnie Merle, which was fine with me. My mother stopped by to see me almost every day, and about three months after the beating, Grandma said it was all right to visit the house on Jackson Street during the day. "You be careful over there, child," she warned. "I don't wanna have to kill that fool."

It seemed to me that Baba had decided to back off some, and if he was at home when I went to see my mother he usually left me alone. He'd find some busywork and just disappear until I left. Still, the visits were always uncomfortable for me, and I always tried to go and see her when he wasn't around.

Minnie and Me

When I wasn't out playing ball or in school, I usually hung out with my uncles and aunts, particularly Minnie Merle. It was during those years, just about the time we entered junior high school, that Minnie and I got to be real good friends. She was outgoing, full of fun, and she had all sorts of friends. I guess I began to depend on her to help me overcome my shyness and develop some kind of social life.

Minnie really loved to dance, and she was up on all the latest music. So on Saturday nights we listened to WLAC, a rhythm and blues radio station broadcast out of Nashville, Tennessee. They had these shows called "Randy's Record Shop" and "Ernie's Record Mart" that played all the latest tunes. One of the DJs was Randy the Horseman. He would play Johnny Ace, Big Mama Thornton, Little Junior Parker, B. B. King, and the Dominoes with Clyde McPhatter. I loved those old tunes like "Sixty Minute Man," "Pledging My Love," and "Hound Dog." We listened to the music, and Minnie would try to show me a few dance steps. I couldn't wait for those Saturday night sessions with her.

By the time I got to junior high school, Minnie would take me with her when she went to the local teenage hangout. It was a funky little joint called Dee's, which was a block down the street from my grandmother's house. They served alcohol, so it wasn't just for teenagers. But in those days they weren't as strict about keeping young people out of places like that, particularly in black neighborhoods in the South. Grandma didn't approve, but whenever we could, Minnie and I would sneak out, go down to Dee's, and play our favorite tunes on the jukebox. Minnie teased me because I always played the same tune. Whenever I got a nickel to play a song, I'd choose Johnny Ace's "Pledging My Love," and Minnie would crack up laughing. I was still pretty shy, but Minnie would bounce around that place talking to everybody; she was full of fun, and she loved to party. Whenever I hung back, she would drag me out on the floor and try to show me how to dance. I loved those nights out with my aunt, and after a while I even started to get over some of my self-consciousness, at least on the dance floor.

Playing ball, of course, was always comfortable for me. It didn't matter whether it was football, basketball, or baseball—by then I'd earned the respect of the guys my age even though I hadn't played any organized ball. Outside of sports, though, when I was on my own I never had as much fun as the times I spent with Minnie.

Losing Charles

In fact, those first few years in junior high school were about the toughest times I faced during my childhood. And it wasn't so much that terrible things were happening to me. No, it was the people close to me. For a while there, it seemed like everything around me started falling apart. The worst, by far, involved my mother's fourth child.

About two years after I began living with my grandmother, my mother and my stepfather had their third baby. His name was Charles, and by the time he was nearly three years old, I had become very close to him. I loved that little guy. See, even though I tried to stay out of Baba's way, I still visited my mother whenever I could, and I'd always spend time with little Charles. My mother knew how much I liked him, so when she was busy or had to do some chores, she'd have me look out for him. Sometimes I would even take him to my grandmother's house, and he'd stay all night. We would sleep in one of the beds with my aunts and uncles, crammed in there like sardines, and he'd hug me all night long. Yeah, I loved my little brother.

Then one day during the spring when I was thirteen, my mother was inside cleaning the house and she left Charles out in the yard. Baba was at his job down at the Bastrop Feed Store, so she told me, Lee Jr., and my sister Dorothy Faye to keep an eye on him. There were pear trees in her backyard, and at that time of year they were still green. I remember her warning us, "Don't let Charles eat those green pears. It'll give him diarrhea."

As usual, I was playing ball, and I guess I wasn't paying much attention to Charles. Somehow, everybody lost track of him. Then about an hour later, my mother came out to look for him. Everybody started rushing around calling out for him, and finally we found him lying under a pear tree. He had been eating those green pears, and he was just lying there whimpering and holding his stomach.

We grabbed him and carried him into the house. At first, my mother thought it was just a stomachache. But that afternoon

27

he started having diarrhea, and it wouldn't stop. Lula Bell called my grandmother and they stayed up all night trying to bring the fever down, but Charles got worse. By daybreak, my mother was really upset. She had done everything she could, but nothing was working. Early that morning, they rushed Charles to Bastrop General Hospital in the truck my stepfather borrowed from the feed store. The nurses said he was dehydrated, but according to my mother, they didn't take it very seriously. They just hooked him up to an IV and left him there.

Charles stayed in that hospital from early morning until five o'clock that afternoon, and a few doctors stopped and looked at him but no one examined him closely. My mother said he was just lying there in the bed suffering. You have to remember that back in those days segregation was at its worst. And in the South, if you were black and as poor as we were, it was difficult to get medical care unless you went to a Negro hospital. So Charles was left there alone, basically ignored. And that evening, he died.

I never got over my brother's death. I still think about it now, and I can't help feeling bad. It was such a waste. I know that in part it's guilt. I'll never forgive myself for letting Charles out of my sight that day. But it's also anger at how things were back in the 1950s. I'm sure that if it had happened today, that child would have survived.

Nothing, of course, compared to losing my little brother, and I was in shock for months. And then, while I was still reeling from Charles's death, some other disappointments made things even rougher.

Losing Minnie

The first setback involved Aunt Minnie. As I said, she was my closest friend, and I was very dependent on her. After Charles died, I think we became even closer. We consoled each other, and I really looked forward to the times we spent hanging out at Dee's. Then a year or so later, I started noticing a change in her. She had gotten very moody, and sometimes when I started jiving around with her like we always did, she would just walk away and say she didn't want to be bothered. One day, while we were getting ready for school at my grandmother's house, I looked out and saw her out in the backyard throwing up. I was worried because I really didn't know what was wrong with her. And when I asked, she wouldn't tell me. A few months later, Minnie dropped out of school. She was in the eighth grade.

Minnie still wouldn't tell me what was wrong, but by that time I suspected that she was going to have a baby. She had been going out with an older guy named Maurice, who was from Cleveland. He was actually the nephew of my uncle Will's wife, Hattie Mae. He came to Bastrop to visit his aunt, and when he met Minnie, he stayed. They had been dating for about six months, and I knew they were tight.

Still, I asked my grandmother why Minnie had quit school, and she finally said, "Well, son, Minnie Merle is pregnant."

At first, I think I truly hated Maurice. Minnie was very smart, and it didn't seem right that she had to leave school. I was sorry for her as well as for myself, because I'd always dreamed that after we graduated from high school, she and I would go to college together. She was the closest friend I had, and I felt that Maurice had come between us and destroyed that friendship. I couldn't imagine going to school every day without her support. As a child, it was one of my biggest disappointments. I was devastated.

Minnie Merle was fifteen when she had her baby, and a year or so later she married Maurice. They stayed in Bastrop for a while, and during that time I got to know him a little better. It took some time, but I finally realized how much he loved her. They moved to Cleveland after I entered the eleventh grade. Later, when I started playing for the Cincinnati Royals, I'd drive up to Cleveland to see them. They were doing well, and we got along fine. But I still couldn't help wondering if Minnie wouldn't have been better off if she had finished school.

Johnnie Mae

I was starting to get interested in girls just before Minnie got pregnant, and when we went to Dee's on weekends, she noticed that I was eyeing some of her girlfriends. She tried to help me out and introduced me to some of them, but I was still too shy to talk to them. I was interested, but I was still just looking. And at Dee's there was plenty to look at. The place was filled with beautiful girls. The one who caught my eye had the smoothest, blackest skin in the world. Her name was Johnnie Mae Taylor. I knew her from school before, but when I saw her laughing and dancing at that joint, I fell in love with her. I never got up the nerve to talk to her or tell her how I felt, but whenever I saw her I hung around, trying to get her to notice me.

I think she knew how I felt, because whenever I was around she would smile and say hello. She never called me "Robert Earl," like everybody else—she called me "Love." She would walk up, blink those big brown eyes, and say, "Hey, Love. What you doing today?" And I would freeze and stand there trying to think of something to say, or, worse, I'd stammer out something silly. I don't think I got out more than one or two coherent sentences during the entire time I knew her. But in my mind, I always had something slick to say, and I dreamed about her all the time.

She was so pretty it hurt. On top of that, she was an excellent athlete. She wasn't a tomboy, but she was good at most sports—better than some of the guys—which was unusual back in the '50s, when women weren't supposed to be athletic. She was a majorette in junior high school, and she loved to play softball. When I saw her marching with the band or playing ball, I couldn't keep my eyes off her. She was about the sweetest thing in my school, just beautiful. She knew she looked good, but Johnnie Mae was a good girl. She wasn't out there talking trash like some of her friends. It seemed to me she was almost as bashful as I was.

I still think she may have liked me a little bit, but I was afraid to say anything, so it never really went any farther than looking at each other. Of course, I was dying to talk to her, but I was afraid I'd just make a fool of myself. When we moved to the next grade, Johnnie Mae had started to really fill out. She was only fourteen, but she was already well developed. And it wasn't long before some of the older guys started to notice her. After that, I knew I didn't have a chance.

A year or so later, she got pregnant by a smooth-talking senior and dropped out of school. That really broke my heart. I guess that's when I began to realize that my stuttering was a serious problem, much more than just a classroom annoyance or some minor quirk that the kids teased me about. I didn't get over Johnnie Mae until I got to high school, and even then I still thought she was the most gorgeous young lady I'd ever seen in my life.

My Grandmother's Strength

Those first two years in junior high school really rocked me. It was the lowest point in my life up until that time. With the death of my little brother, and Minnie and Johnnie Mae getting pregnant and dropping out of school, I just fell apart. I couldn't understand why all these things were happening to the people I loved. And for a while there, I started feeling sorrow for myself. I felt inadequate, and sometimes I just couldn't hide it. If my grandmother hadn't been there to support me, I don't know what I would've done.

There were times when I'd start out to school with the rest of the kids and then turn around and go back home. When that happened or when I'd return home from school shaking and crying on days when I couldn't laugh off the wisecracks and jokes, I went straight to my grandmother. I knew I could count on her. She would always pull me into her arms and comfort me. And when she did, there was one thing she told me over and over. "Robert Earl," she'd say, "wasn't but one perfect person walked this earth. Everybody got a handicap or disability. I don't care who they are. The thing is, you gotta have a dream,

31

son. You gotta have a dream and you got to keep it. You got to
hold on to your dream. No matter how bad things may look."
She must have told me that a hundred times; and of all the
things she ever said to me, that was the advice I remembered
most.

She was an amazing woman. She had a soft, loving side that
was as tender and caring as I've ever seen in a woman. But she
was also strong. Strong willed. Strong minded. Most of the
time she was easygoing and friendly, but she could be fiercely
independent and stubborn. I saw her defy people that most
black folks wouldn't dare challenge, and I don't remember her
ever backing down to anybody when she thought she was right.
Nothing frightened that woman. I had learned that a few years
earlier when my grandfather told me about the time she stood
up to the whole town of Bastrop.

According to Grandpa, back in the early '40s Ella Mae gathered all her children together one day and warned them to stay
away from town the next day. "They goin' lynch a colored man
tomorrow," she told them. "It's goin' be dangerous."

Grandpa had a habit of livening up stories and stretching
the facts, but the way he told it, Ella Mae went downtown by
herself the next day. She told everybody else to stay at home,
and walked into town wearing her best cotton dress and a hat
and purse that she only wore on Sundays when she went to
church. When she arrived, a few people had already started
milling around the county courthouse. Soon a crowd gathered,
and they were hooting and hollering as if they were at a picnic.
A few of them wore white hoods and robes. By the time I heard
the tale, I'd seen folks dressed exactly like that riding through
our own neighborhood at night, and I knew he was talking
about the Ku Klux Klan.

32   That day, Ella Mae was the only black person in town. She
was down there all by herself, standing at the edge of the crowd.
They couldn't help but notice her, since she towered above most
of the folks surrounding her. A few turned and glared at her, but
she didn't flinch, he said, just ignored them and held her ground.
She stood there straight as a rod, eyes fixed on the courthouse

lawn and the oak tree with a rope dangling from a limb, looking as dignified and proud as she could be.

Then they dragged this black man out toward the big oak tree that still stands on the courthouse lawn. He didn't look to be much older than some of the high school students at Morehouse, Grandpa said. The crowd rushed at him, stripped his shirt away, and started clubbing and pushing him toward a big crate that had been placed under the tree. When they got him up on the crate, someone put a hood over his head. Then they stood him up on the crate and slipped the rope around his neck. People started shouting, "Kill 'em! Kill 'em!" And somebody kicked the crate away. There was a loud gasp and a minute of silence. Then the mob began cheering and yelling. They went wild, everybody started shouting and jumping up and down just like they'd watched someone throw a touchdown pass at a football game. Everybody except Ella Mae.

She stood there silently, stone-faced, Grandpa said. Didn't move one inch from her spot at the edge of that crowd. She just kept her eyes riveted on the black man dangling from the tree. Then something peculiar happened. Sensing her presence, a few people started moving away from her. They didn't know what to make of this bold black woman standing there in the middle of their lynch party. Grandpa said the folks nearest her stopped cheering and just stared at her. Ella Mae looked at them and shook her head. Then, just like she was talking to me or one of her children, she said, "You white people ought to be shame of yo'self . . . ought to be shamed." Up front, where the black man was swinging from the tree, they were still yelling and cheering, but the people around her fell silent. When she turned and started to walk away, they just stepped aside. Nobody said a word to her or tried to stop her, and she walked out of town just as calmly as she had walked in there.

Now, I can't vouch for all the facts of Grandpa's tale. All I know is that people say there was a lynching about that time and that Ella Mae never denied it. I do know that Grandma didn't take anything from anybody. Didn't take no mess. When she thought she was right, she just wouldn't back down. I truly

33

respected that woman—wanted to be just like her. I guess I admired her strength and determination more than anything else. She was one of the most determined people I ever met. And while I may have slipped up a few times trying to live up to her Christian ethics and principles, I learned something else from her that stuck with me forever.

Ella Mae was the hardest-working, most self-reliant person I've ever known. "If you want somethin', don't expect nobody to give it to you," she'd say. "You got to get out and work for it." That was one her favorite sayings. But it wasn't just her saying it that impressed me and everyone else who knew her. It was the way she struggled, sacrificed, and always found a way to eke out enough money to keep the family going. She just wouldn't give up. Even today, whenever I struggle or face some serious challenge, I try to imagine how she might react.

I guess she always had some kind of odd job that helped make ends meet by supplementing Grandpa's retirement check, but I didn't really notice how hard she worked until I reached my teens. That's when she started working at the Bastrop Paper Mill. She worked in the mill's kitchen during breakfast and lunch. She had to be there before six o'clock to help prepare breakfast for the early shift. There were no buses then, so she got up at four o'clock in the morning and walked the five miles to the mill. Sometimes I'd wake up when I heard her leaving and sneak over to the window to watch. On cold mornings, I'd see her all bundled up as she tiptoed out the door. It was always pitch black outside, and I'd watch her disappear into the darkness before I went back to sleep. Still, in the afternoon when I got home from school, she was always there waiting to greet us as if she had been there all day. She worked there for years, and I never heard her complain once.

34   Ella Mae also had a kind of tenant farmer arrangement with one of the plantation owners down in Oak Ridge. She leased a plot of land every year and raised cotton. During the summer, she took a two-week vacation from her mill job and had me and a few of her own kids help with the picking. We worked our tails off, stayed out in the fields from sunup to sundown. And

by the end of that two weeks, we'd have the whole crop piled up in a big wagon. Grandma would have someone bring a tractor and haul it down to the gin.

After it was sold and she had paid the plantation owner, Grandma went straight to the bank and paid as much as she could on the house mortgage. There was never very much money left, but she always gave me and my aunts and uncles five dollars each for helping with the picking. The rest went for groceries and clothes for the kids. We looked forward to those two weeks, because afterward we had a little pocket change and we ate a little better than we did during the winter. It was hard work, but nobody complained. Grandma worked right along with us, and she would always remind us that if you want something, you had to work hard for it. She kept telling us, "You got to do it for yo'self."

It was my grandmother's encouragement, strength, and advice that got me through my early teens. Working hard and never letting go of my dreams were the goals she hammered into my mind. And during the times when I was at my lowest, I tried to draw on her advice.

My Escape in Sports

By the time I reached the eighth grade, I knew I was a pretty good athlete. I could run, jump, and perform in most sports as well as or better than all the other kids. So I turned to sports as a way of blanking out the grief and disappointment that I felt about Charles, Minnie, and Johnnie Mae, and all of the frustration I felt about my speech problem. When playing ball, I never felt inadequate.

During the week, after I came home from school, I'd either go out to the backyard and practice football and basketball by myself or join the other guys in pickup games. We didn't have a park with real facilities, but there was a big empty lot about a quarter of a mile down the street from my grandmother's house, and that was where we played baseball and football. We had to walk over to the Morehouse campus if we wanted to play basketball. There was no inside gym at that time, but sometimes we could play on the same dirt court that the high school team used to play their games. The competition was rough. And since the older guys would always run us off the court when they wanted to play, the kids my age usually wound up playing football or baseball at the empty lot.

I guess those days practicing in the backyard with that rolled-up newspaper had worked, because by the time I was thirteen I'd become a very good football player. All my buddies told me that I should go out for the team, and in the ninth grade I decided to give it a try.

4

HIGH SCHOOL HOOP DREAMS

It may sound crazy, but I wanted to be the
Beethoven of basketball.

WENT OUT FOR FOOTBALL in the ninth grade and made the team as a second-string quarterback. I didn't become a starter until the following year. And that came as a surprise to a lot of the guys. See, everybody laughed when I said I was going out for quarterback. The older players, juniors and seniors, cracked up. "Man, how you goin' play quarterback," they said. "You can't call no plays—take you two days just to say hello."

Even my friend Bullet, who was in my class, teased me. We hung out and played football together, and we were always big rivals in sports. Both of us wanted to be quarterbacks, and despite the friendship, the competition was heated. He couldn't believe it when I beat him out and made first team in my sophomore year. The thing was, although I had some trouble communicating, I could usually compensate with my athletic skills. I was an excellent passer, and when a play broke down I was fast enough to scramble and run the ball.

I had the strongest arm out there. At the time, I could throw the ball over 100 yards. I threw that thing from end zone to end zone. That was back in 1958, and, as I said before, my favorite player was Johnny Unitas. I dreamed about being just like him. I wanted to be the greatest quarterback in the world. Although our coach, William Washington, had some reservations about my ability to lead the team, he never questioned my athletic skills or my enthusiasm. Before each game, he'd call me over and say, "Don't worry about the calls, son, we can help you with that. Just go out and play like I know you can." I really respected that man, and I tried to never let him down.

I guess that subconsciously, even back then I wanted to do something that required speaking. But all during the time I played quarterback for Morehouse, I stuttered so badly that I was ashamed to speak. It was awful. In the classroom, I always had a great understanding for things I read. If you told me something or I read it, I never forgot it, and I always did well on examinations. But when they called on somebody to read or answer a question or recite something from a lesson, my heart would start pumping a hundred miles an hour. I'd duck down and hide behind the person sitting in front of me. All day long, I sat there praying that classes would end. I couldn't wait for the bell to ring, for anything to happen to get me out of the classroom.

It was another story on the football field. A lot of people never understood how I did it. And when I look back at it, I can understand why. After all, in the 1960s a 6-foot 6-inch quarterback was unusual, and it must have been odd seeing somebody my size, particularly someone who stuttered as badly as I did, calling plays and running a football team. Still, I don't remember ever getting called for running out the clock because of my speech problem. Somehow, my adrenaline started running, and I always managed to stammer out the plays on time. Not that there weren't some close calls.

A lot of times I would go in the huddle and get stuck on a number. But all my teammates would start hitting me on the back or slapping me upside the helmet. "C'mon, Robert Earl! This ain't no time to be foolin' 'round," they'd yell. "Spit it out, man." Then we would rush up to the line and barely get the play off before the clock expired.

38 All the guys would come back to the huddle and laugh about it. And, of course, after the game I was the butt of all the jokes. But I loved it and those guys respected me for the way I played. They were my teammates, and we were really tight. The jokes and teasing may even have brought us closer, because when we were out partying after a game and someone else started getting

on me, they were always right there to defend me. Being a part of that football team, playing with those guys, was a great experience. We won the state championship in football during my sophomore and junior years at Morehouse. And in my senior year we lost by just one point in the championship game. We were playing against T. A. Levy, a good team from a little town near Baton Rouge; and on the last play of that game, I threw a pass that bounced out of the hands of our fullback just as he stepped into the end zone. If he could have held on, we would have had a threepeat. We were disappointed but after the game no one said a word. He was a great player and without him, we would have never gotten that far in the tournament.

The Effects of Segregation

We had great teams, and the whole community supported us. Some of them didn't like us, but they still rooted for us. Black schools never competed against white schools in Louisiana during that time. We played in separate divisions and had separate tournaments. The white high school in Bastrop was bigger because they brought in students from the outlying areas, but we always had better athletic teams. The white kids knew it, and they always came to see us play. Of course, they weren't allowed to come in and sit with the black fans. Black folks didn't really care, but Jim Crow laws worked both ways; there were BLACK ONLY and WHITE ONLY signs all over town. Nearly all public facilities were segregated. Still, a lot of high school kids came and stood outside the fences to watch the games. Sometimes, when there was a real important game, even a few adults would sneak out to watch us.

That was just about a decade after the color line had been broken in professional athletics, and black superstars like Jackie Robinson, Larry Doby, Willie Mays, and a few others had made names for themselves in baseball. Jim Brown had started tearing up the NFL, and Bill Russell, Wilt Chamberlain, and Elgin Baylor were big stars in basketball. Even in the South, white kids were starting to root for black athletes. All that race stuff was forgotten when they came out to support us on the football field or basketball court. When we saw them out there cheering, we'd wave at them and they'd wave back at us. Mandatory school integration, sit-ins, and freedom rides were just starting, and the tension was high in the South; but despite all the problems, sports was a bridge between blacks and whites. Most of the kids got along; there wasn't a lot of hate between young whites and blacks. Everybody did their own thing and went their own way, but I felt that many of them admired us.

It was too bad that they had all those barriers back in those days. I think that if we'd competed against each other in sports, we would have gotten to know each other sooner, and a lot of the problems could have been avoided. The way it was, there were always barriers. They allowed the white kids to come and watch us play, and nobody said anything. But whenever we tried to go and watch a game at the white school, the police would come and run us off.

My Growing Interest in Basketball

Football was great, but I always thought of myself as an all-around athlete. I loved all sports. I was always skinny, but besides being able to throw the football a mile, I could also jump and I was fast. I was even pretty good at baseball until I started facing guys who threw eighty miles an hour. After that I was a little leery about stepping up to the plate. But basketball had always been one my favorites, and since I was so tall, guys kept telling me that I should take it more seriously. And as I grew up and watched our school teams, I knew that someday I wanted to play for the varsity. Even after I made the football team and we won the championship, I was drawn to basketball.

We had a few lots where we played ball, and they were all grass and dirt. That was fine for baseball and football, but it didn't work as well for basketball. Our school didn't get an indoor gym until I reached eighth grade. The old court was outside near the football field. For most of my childhood, even the high school basketball team played on an outdoor court with packed-down dirt, and players would slip and slide all over the place. Thinking about it now, it must have given Morehouse an advantage. The ball was slick and hard to handle, and the footing was treacherous. Opposing teams had a hard time adjusting.

I guess I started getting more interested in basketball while watching those outdoor games in my preteens. The facilities were poor, but we had some great teams, and our uniforms were terrific. The warm-up jackets were made out of this satin-like material that looked just like pro warm-ups; the pants and jackets were gold with blue stripes. They were beautiful. And the uniforms were just as slick. What got me, though, were the shoes. They had two sets of shoes, one blue and one gold. When the team came out in those uniforms with long white socks and either the gold or the blue shoes, everybody was impressed. I know I envied those guys from the first moment I saw them.

It was peculiar, but despite the Jim Crow laws and segregated schools, our sports teams were dressed and equipped as well as the white schools. Our football and baseball teams also had beautiful uniforms (though not as fancy as the basketball uniforms) and all the bats, gloves, balls, pads, and protective equipment we needed. It always seemed strange to me, almost as though they wanted to keep black and white kids separated so badly that they made sure blacks didn't have anything to complain about. That may have been why they finally built an indoor gym in the mid-'50s, just as the push for school desegregation started to heat up. I'm sure that's why they built a swimming pool for blacks a few years later.

Of course, at that age I wasn't concerned about reasons or motives—my interest started shifting from football to basketball when I saw those uniforms and watched those guys play. I was already a pretty good football player, and everybody knew it. But I sensed that I could also excel in basketball. That's when I nailed the coat-hanger hoop onto the house, made a ball out of my grandfather's old sock, and started practicing in the backyard. I was out there day and night, before school and after school. And I found a pickup game whenever I could.

It wasn't always easy, because I was the only guy in my immediate neighborhood who was really serious about sports. Nearly everybody else seemed more interested in schoolwork, music, or the arts. The best athletes lived north of me on the other side of the pulp ditch. So when I wanted to get into a real competitive game, I'd walk across town to their neighborhood. Although a lot of guys didn't have gym shoes, we had some terrific games. Most of us wore our street shoes, but a few kids played in their bare feet. It was wild. Guys would be slipping and falling down, and since it was hard to stop, everybody got called for traveling. Still, we had some great players out there. It was typical playground-style ball with a lot of freelancing and hot-dogging. We were all trying to hang and float like Elgin Baylor. That's where I picked up a lot of the moves that I'd eventually use in college and the NBA.

When I started, I was one of the guys who played in street shoes. I had these big old high-top brogues, and it felt like I was wearing weights on my feet. It was a definite handicap, since most of the best ballplayers had sneakers. Even though I was just learning the game, I was doing all right against those guys. After a while, though, I realized that I'd have to have some sneakers if I wanted to improve.

My grandmother barely had enough money for the regular shoes I got at West Bros. Dry Goods Store, and I knew she couldn't afford gym shoes. But when I talked with my brother, he told me to ask my stepfather for money to buy sneakers. Before asking him, I went downtown and checked out shoes at West Bros. From the start, I had my eyes on these PF Flyers. But I knew that even if Baba gave me the money, he wasn't about to pay any more than he had to for some sneakers. So when I asked him, I said I needed $1.99, which was the cost of the cheapest shoes in the store.

He wasn't happy about giving me anything, but finally he handed me a five dollar bill and said, "Don't spend a cent more than $1.99." I nodded yes. And as I walked out of the door, he yelled, "I mean it, boy. Bring back every bit of my change."

When I left, I had every intention of buying those cut-rate sneakers. But when I got to the store, I started wavering. I looked at the $1.99 shoes, and all of a sudden they looked pretty shabby. The salesman kept telling me how much better the PF Flyers were, and the more he talked the better they looked. I don't know what got into me, but even though I knew I was going to catch hell when I got home, I bought the PF Flyers. They only cost $2.50, but I knew my stepfather was going to pitch a fit when I gave him his change.

It was early afternoon when I left the store, and I was scared to death. I was afraid to go home, so I spent the day hanging out with a couple of my friends. It was near dark when I finally got up enough nerve to face my stepfather and give him his money. I walked in and put the change on the table. But before I could get out of the door and return to my grandmother's house, he picked up the money and saw that I'd only left $2.50. I was standing at the door shaking. At first, I thought he was going to come at me, but instead he just stared at me with a look that would have killed an elephant. Finally, he yelled, "Boy, don't ever ask me for another dime. Get out of my house. I can't even stand to look at you."

My stepfather didn't give me another penny after that day. He never bought anything for me, and as a matter of fact, I never asked him for anything. We didn't speak much before he picked up and moved to Los Angeles with Lula Bell and their kids. They didn't ask me to go with them, but at the time I didn't mind. I was about to begin my sophomore year in high school. I wanted to play football, and I was perfectly happy staying with grandmother. And with those gym shoes I went out for the junior high basketball team, and I fell in love with the game that eventually became the source of my livelihood: basketball.

Working the Fields

I did all right on the junior high school team. But because I was also playing football, basketball remained a secondary interest for a while. Then, too, it was the late 1950s and a whole lot of things were going on in the country. It wasn't apparent in our little town, but all over the South there were rumblings about

43

change, civil rights, and freedom. I heard talk about Martin Luther King Jr. and protests, about Thurgood Marshall, Arkansas's Governor Faubus, President Eisenhower, and the trouble in Little Rock. There was even some joking about how long it would be before we started playing against the white schools—but while I was in Bastrop, not much changed. Things went along pretty much the same way they had since I was a child.

Like a lot of my friends, I chopped and picked cotton all through high school. For black kids who wanted work, those were practically the only jobs available. During the summer, June to August, the cotton had to be chopped or weeded. Then, from late August to November, we would pick and put it in big sacks. Every morning before dawn during the cotton season, the owners of the big plantations would send a caravan of a dozen or so large flatbed trucks with wooden side rails into town. Everybody who wanted to go out and work would gather in front of J. D.'s Grocery Store. So at about four o'clock each morning, a whole gang of black folks would be milling around waiting to get a chance to earn some money. Usually, the white truck drivers took nearly everybody who showed up; the only people they left behind were a few old folks who seemed too feeble to work or some little kids who looked like they should have stayed at home with their mamas. They would load hundreds of people onto those trucks and drive us out to the fields. Some plantations were ten to twenty miles away, and by the time we got there the sun would be coming up.

During the picking season, with football practice and school and helping my grandmother with her own little cotton plot, I could only work in the fields occasionally. But I tried to work every day during the summer, when we chopped. As soon as we arrived and got off the trucks, they gave us a hoe and sent us out to the fields. Each person had his or her own row, and we had to try to straighten it out and make sure that there was enough space around each plant. They wanted us to remove all the weeds and grass from around the plants and keep the row nice and neat. It was much harder than just picking cotton because you had to use a lot of elbow grease, and by the end of the day your hands would be callused and cut up. It was hard, backbreaking work.

We usually started at about six o'clock and worked until noon, when there was a one-hour lunch break. Then we went back to the fields and worked until five o'clock. It was hot out there. The sun was blistering hot and it felt like your skin was being scorched by a thousand branding irons. Not everybody made it through the day, and if you didn't show up after lunch or couldn't keep up, the man would come and take back the hoe. You were out of there, and those who left early didn't ride back to town. Once I got out there, I never quit. But by the end of the day, my arms and shoulders would be aching, and sometimes my hands were bleeding. Most of the time, I was so tired I felt like collapsing on the spot.

Everybody stopped at five o'clock, and the boss stood and watched as we lined up to get back on the trucks. We returned the hoes, and when we dropped them on a pile near the trucks, he paid each of us two dollars and fifty cents. You didn't get paid unless you returned that hoe. During the ride back to town, we were always exhausted, but it felt good having a little bit of change in your pocket. And by the time I got home, I was revived. I wanted to go out and enjoy it.

Before I did anything else, I always gave my grandmother two dollars from the money I'd earned. Then most days I'd go to the well and haul back water to fill up the tub so I could take a bath. After that I always went straight to J. D.'s Grocery Store. The days when I worked in the fields were the only times that I had extra money to get myself some food or any kind of treat like sweets or candy, and I couldn't wait to get to the store.

I had to save enough of the fifty cents that was left to buy lunch the next day, but since it seemed like I was always hungry, I usually wound up spending half my money on food on those evenings. I'd buy a can of pork and beans or sardines and some crackers. Then I'd get a big bottle of grape or orange Nehi pop and one of those gingerbread cakes with cream filling and chocolate icing on the outside. All of that cost about

45

thirty-five cents, so I'd have a little left for lunch when I went back to the fields the next day. I'd come back home and stuff myself. And when there was something left over, I would carefully wrap it up in a paper bag and put it in the icebox. You couldn't leave anything out because during the night the roaches came out, and they would be all over it. As soon as we put out the lamplights before going to sleep, they came out of hiding. If you woke during the night and lit one of the lamps, they would be climbing over everything. As soon as the light came on, those suckers would tear off and scurry back into the cracks along the walls. That was all part of life when I grew up in Bastrop. It was a reality for most of the poor people that I knew back there.

Morehouse Varsity Basketball

Although I played in a lot of pickup games and had started to get much better at the game, I didn't go out for the varsity basketball team until I got to the eleventh grade. The older guys, who had played together since junior high, weren't thrilled about an upstart stepping in to join them, so I sat out during that first year. I really didn't want to get into a hassle with them. I guess they felt that since I was the quarterback on the football team and hadn't proven myself in basketball, I'd mess up the chemistry on the team. They were good, and since they'd played together for so long, all of them knew what the others could do. They had a tight-knit unit and everybody really blended together well. Still, the summer before my junior year, the basketball coach, Payne Montgomery, saw me playing and asked me to come out for the team.

46   Once I started practicing with the team, the seniors accepted me pretty quickly. I'd always felt that I was one of the best athletes in my school, so I wasn't intimidated. Still, I had to prove myself, and they didn't cut me any slack. I was raw and skinny (180 pounds and about 6 feet 6 inches), but when they saw that I could run and jump and shoot with the best of them, I think

they realized that I would be an asset. I started the year coming off the bench as the sixth man, and by the end of the season I even started a few games. We had a hell of a team with some great athletes that year.

Our center was Lucious Jackson, who went on to play for Pan American College and the Philadelphia 76ers. He was 6 feet 9 inches and about 250 pounds back in high school, and he was a monster on the boards and in the pivot. Then we had Bob Brown, who played forward and center. Bob was about 6 feet 6 inches and weighed 270 pounds. We called him Highway because he had to walk about seven miles each way to get to school, and guys would tease him about having big, flat feet. Bob was a terrific guy, and after college he went on to play football for the Green Bay Packers. There were some great athletes in our school.

The team's other star was a guy named Albert Johnson—we called him Ham. Lucious and Ham led the team in scoring. Each of them averaged over 20 points a game. I only averaged 8 points and 5 rebounds a game, but with those guys as the frontline and me coming off the bench, we were practically unbeatable. We went on to win the state championship in my junior year. It was a terrific year for the school and for me. Morehouse won the state championship in football and basketball, and I was part of both of those teams.

My game improved immensely that year, and a lot of the improvement came from playing with and against guys like Ham. He was a great high school basketball player. He had all kinds of moves. He could handle the ball, and when he played outside he was so deceptive that it seemed like he was by you before you knew what happened—had a great first step. On top of that, he was a great shooter, and if he decided to, he could post you up. When he got you on his back in the pivot, you were at his mercy. But Ham was rough and kind of dirty; you know, always pushing and throwing elbows. If he thought he could get away with it, he'd punish you, try to intimidate you.

Most of the guys on the playgrounds were a little afraid of Ham, and in pickup games nobody wanted to guard him. The

47

thing is, even when I started playing basketball, I wasn't afraid of anyone. I thought I could play against the best, so Ham didn't frighten me. And since he was one of the best ballplayers in the area, I jumped at the chance to guard him. It was a true challenge for me, and I knew I'd improve if I faced up to it.

That wasn't easy. Ham was only 6 feet 3 inches, but he weighed about 190 pounds. He was a lean, muscular kid. And to me, it always looked as though he had some devious thought in his mind. I think he liked scaring people. Even when he walked around in school he had an intimidating look on his face. I don't think he got off on actually hurting anybody, but he sure enjoyed making everyone think that he did. He would strut around the schoolyard glaring at folks, then laughing when they backed off. Nearly every day during recess, he would walk over to the elementary school where the little kids played and razz them or thump 'em on the head. He was always messing with somebody.

A couple of times when we first played against each other in pickup games, it got real tense. We never actually got into a fight, but we had a few tussles. Ham loved faking his opponent, getting him to leap up in the air over his back and then, when he went up for his shot, slamming him with an elbow. Afterwards, he would yell, "Hey, man, that's a foul on you." He was rough and smart, knew all the little tricks that threw you off your game—sneaky elbows, hipping you out of position, pushing with his forearm, or grabbing your trunks and stepping on your feet. You had to watch out for everything when you played against Ham. He was always testing you.

It wasn't long after we started playing against each other that Ham and I had our first hassle. We were playing in the school-yard when he drove and faked a shot. I went up to block it, and he moved under me. When I came down on his back, he gave me a shot with his elbow, pivoted, and made a bank shot. He laughed, but he caught me in the stomach and it hurt. I was angry and a little embarrassed, but I was determined not to fall for it again. A few minutes later, when he tried the same move,

I didn't go for the fake. I waited. Although he was heavier and stronger, I had a few inches on him, and when he spun to put up the shot I slapped it out of bounds. It was a clean block, but he was furious.

He yelled, "Foul," and grabbed the ball.

I just smiled and said, "All right."

Next time down the court, he tried that same move. I blocked the shot again, and this time when he came down, he slapped me in the face. I thought it was intentional, and I was mad. So I told him not to do it again. The very next time down the court Ham went up again; he was determined to beat me. This time he tried a different move; he feinted to his left and then to his right before spinning for his shot. When I blocked it, he screamed foul again. This time I disputed his call, and we got into a heated argument. We started pushing and shoving each other, and a few of the other players had to step in to break it up.

We never did really fight, and after that incident we became pretty good friends. Ham always wanted me on his team because I was basically the only guy who wasn't afraid of him. He knew I could play, and I began realizing how much I enjoyed facing the challenge of competing against really good ballplayers. The funny thing is, when I went out for the varsity, Ham was one of my biggest supporters.

In my senior year, I made the starting team. But Lucious, Ham, and Bob Brown had graduated, and our team wasn't as dominant. I averaged 28 points a game that year, but we lost in the second round of the state tournament. Still, I'd had a great year. I was selected to the All-State teams in both football and basketball.

The Influence of My Coaches

My high school days were among the most enjoyable times of my life. I was on top of the world. Like most teenagers, I didn't have a lot of responsibilities. It was mostly good times and having fun. And it seemed that the applause, adoration, and smooth sailing would go on forever. Although I still wasn't dating and didn't have much of a social life, I didn't worry about it. I even forgot about my speech problem. I just lost myself in the excitement of athletics and winning. Everything else seemed unimportant, just minor annoyances; and when some small obstacle did arise, it seemed as though something or somebody would come along and take care of it. For me, those were truly the good old days.

Of course, there was the problem of being black and poor in the South during that time. But there was so much love and joy in my grandmother's house that it was easy to forget just how poor we were. I was often hungry, though, even when I was on cloud nine because of sports. Most of the time, since I'd grown up with very little food, I just ignored it. And by the time I got to high school, I guess I'd gotten used to being a little underfed.

Once, during my junior year in high school, it got to be a serious problem. The football season had begun when I started getting pains in my chest and the lower part of my stomach. At first, everybody thought I might have heart trouble. But it didn't seem that serious to me, and if they had allowed me I would have probably played right through it. But Coach Washington saw me bent over clutching my stomach one day after practice and asked what was wrong. I told him about the pain, and he insisted that I go and see a doctor.

The next day, he took me in for an examination with his doctor. That's when I discovered that I was suffering from malnutrition. When I told them what I ate on a typical day, they were shocked. The doctor couldn't believe I was able to play football living on the kind of diet I'd grown up with at home.

After that, until I graduated and left for college, Coach Washington and my basketball coach, Payne Montgomery, took me under their wings. Those men stepped in and groomed me; they had a tremendous influence on my life. They arranged for me to come to their houses and do little chores around the yard three or four times a week. I'd mow the lawn or clean up the flower beds or rake the leaves. When I finished with the work, they would invite me inside and feed me. I ate better than I had all of my life during that year, and when I went home in the evenings, they would usually give me a bag to take some food back for my aunts and uncles. I really believe that those meals helped make my senior year the best year I'd had in high school sports. And I'm certain that influenced my decision to major in food and nutrition in college. Growing up poor and battling malnutrition will give you a healthy respect for good food. To this day, I have an obsession with eating well.

The Effects of Desegregation

The racial situation was also heating up during my senior year in high school. By 1960, it seemed like everybody was protesting, and there were demonstrations and riots all over the country. That was the year the Student Nonviolent Coordinating Committee was founded over at Shaw University in North Carolina, and shortly afterward, Martin Luther King Jr. joined with that group to step up the sit-in protests. We didn't see much of anything, but we heard about all the commotion. Later that year, in our own state a judge ordered New Orleans schools to desegregate. And although very little happened in Bastrop, you could sense the tension building. It seemed as though everybody thought a change was coming. Some people looked forward to it, and some were scared. But nobody knew what to expect.

As it turned out, a few years after I left, there were some changes. And most of them were for the better. Schools and things like the movies and other public facilities were desegregated, some jobs opened up, and blacks didn't have to always walk on tiptoes around white folks. But it seemed to me that a lot of changes hurt blacks. Before the Jim Crow barriers came down, a lot of black people in my area owned their own businesses. They had restaurants, nightclubs, a few grocery stores, a taxi cab company, and a little shuttle bus company that picked up the kids who lived too far out in the country to walk to

51

school; they even had their own radio station. Except for a few juke joints down on the Block, all those things have disappeared. When everybody rushed in to take advantage of integration, they stopped supporting black-owned businesses. We became totally dependent on white people. It seemed like a setback to me.

future Promise

But even with my health problems and the social unrest and commotion, those were good times for me. It was during my senior year that I first realized I had a talent that would take me away from Bastrop and shape my future.

Our high school music teacher, Delarose DuBose, was a stern, articulate, no-nonsense woman who really loved the arts. Every day in her class, we'd discuss the history of music, and she'd talk about the contributions of great artists and musicians. She was an intelligent, refined woman, and everybody respected her. She also happened to be a big sports fan. One day in her classroom, during the basketball season, she was telling us about composers like Beethoven, Wagner, and Mozart. "They were exceptional artists," she said. "They had talent and beautiful minds, and like many great artists, they were unlike most other people."

Then she stopped and looked toward the back of the class, and saw me ducking down in my seat, hoping she wouldn't call on me. She paused, then looked back at the class. "You may not know this," she said, "but we have a great artist right here in our class."

Everybody started whispering and looking around the room. She said, "Robert Love is an artist. Have you noticed how he floats to the basket, or glides from one side of the rim to the other, hanging in midair? How he changes his shot at the last minute, and slides between defenders? How he jumps over the heads of other players, or how beautifully he sails toward the basket and dunks?" She looked at me and smiled. "Robert Love is a very unusual person," she said. "He is gifted. On the basketball court, he's as smooth and flawless as the men we've been talking about. He is an artist."

When she finished, everyone in that room turned around to look at me. A few smiled and applauded, but some just stared in disbelief and gasped, "Robert Love? But Robert Love stutters!" I don't think I really heard much after that. I felt this strange glow come over me, and I sat up in my seat and smiled at our teacher. I was so proud, I felt like I was going to burst wide open. That was the day I started truly believing that I was special, that my athletic gift might allow me to prove that I was an exceptional person.

I got home about four o'clock that afternoon, and I couldn't wait to get out to the backyard to practice. Mrs. DuBose's speech had inspired me, and I was determined to show everyone that she was right. By that time, I'd nailed a rim onto a big piece of plywood and hung it on a pole in our neighbor's backyard. I had a basketball that I'd won as Most Valuable Player in a local tournament. I went out there with my old beat-up basketball, and I must have played from four o'clock that afternoon until nine at night. I didn't stop until it got dark. I was driving, pulling up for jump shots, double-clutching and shooting scoop shots and finger rolls, hanging in the air and throwing down monster dunks, backward and forward. It got so good to me that I got into a rhythm. I could hear music that sounded like a symphony, and behind that I heard the sound of the crowd.

That day changed my life. I had practiced and dreamed about playing against the pros for years, but out there in my backyard that night, I knew that I was going to excel in the basketball world. After that, it was almost as if I were obsessed. I dreamed about playing college and professional basketball. Just as I had since I was a child, I'd turn on my grandmother's old radio whenever a game was broadcast at night, and I pictured myself out there with those guys. I just let my imagination run wild, and I could see myself on the court with them. It was so real I

53

could taste it. I never lost. I beat them every time. I saw myself playing against the five greatest basketball players alive, and none of them could stop me or keep up with me. Not Pettit, Chamberlain, Robertson, Russell, or Baylor—no one. In my mind, I dominated them. I beat them every time.

I was determined to be the artist Mrs. DuBose said I was. It may sound crazy, but I wanted to be the Beethoven of basketball.

College Calls

By the spring of my senior year, I began getting some letters and a few calls from college recruiters. I really felt fortunate that they were interested. There were about eighty kids in my class, and a lot of them left the area right after graduation. But most of them just took off and headed north looking for more opportunities and better jobs. I don't think more than ten went to college.

Of course, when my mother and grandmother found out that I had a few scholarship offers, they were thrilled. If I could make it, I'd be the first member of my family to get more than a high school education. When I took the letters and showed them to my family, my grandmother would say, "See that, son, I knew you was going to be something special. That's what happens when you keep your eye on the prize. Lord knows, you gotta have a dream."

I was as proud as I could be, even though there was no stampede to offer me a scholarship. During the late '50s and early '60s, colleges didn't chase after black athletes the way they do today. Most big-time schools didn't even look our way. There were no offers of jobs, big cars, or gratuities by alumni. Northern universities didn't pay much attention to black athletes from the South, and major southern schools were mostly segregated, so they completely ignored us. Even All-State high school players like Lucious Jackson and Willis Reed were passed over and finally ended up at small schools in the South.

54

I think I got one letter from an integrated school in Delaware, but like Lucious and Willis, I focused on offers from black colleges in the South. I considered a few schools that had called or written, but finally it came down to Grambling, my high school basketball coach's alma mater, and Southern University, my football coach's old college. I visited both schools, and just before graduation I chose Southern, which was in Scotlandsville, Louisiana, a little town just outside of Baton Rouge.

5

SOUTHERN COMFORT

I was on top of the world.

ARRIVED AT SOUTHERN UNIVERSITY in June 1961. Since they wanted me to play football and basketball, I had to be there early for summer football workouts. But during the first day of practice with the team, I decided that college football wasn't for me.

The improvement I'd shown during my last year in high school and my music teacher's praise had me leaning toward basketball before I got to Southern, and once I stepped on the field with the football team my mind was pretty much made up. I was a little light even for high school football, and at 6 feet 7 inches and 185 pounds, I felt like a featherweight at Southern. The guys on the team seemed gigantic. Many of them were just as tall as I was, and most weighed about 80 or 90 pounds more than I did. I felt like a skinny little sapling out there with a bunch of oak trees.

After the first week, I went to the coach and told him I wanted to stick with basketball. He agreed, and the next day I turned in my football gear and started hanging out at the gym. The basketball team at Southern had struggled during the previous few years, and I knew that I could make a real contribution. Basketball practice didn't start until the fall, so most of the starters had not arrived. Still, I spent a lot of time in the gym, and I got to know a few of the basketball players who, like me, had summer jobs.

Making Myself at Home

I fell in love with Scotlandsville and Southern's campus that summer. The place was beautiful, and since my job was to mow the lawns, trim the shrubbery, and weed the grounds, I got to know it very well. The college was set on a hill on the outskirts of Scotlandsville, an all-black town that was a suburb of Baton Rouge. It was a small working-class town with a quiet section called Southern Heights where most of the school's professors and staff lived.

The university had about two dozen buildings spread out across its large campus, about 200 acres, and the grounds were dotted with oak trees and weeping willows. From the hilltop, you could look down at the Mississippi River and see barges, small yachts, and pleasure boats floating past. It was one of the most peaceful spots on campus, and later, when I was attending classes and reading books like *Huckleberry Finn*, I spent a lot of time up there sitting on the benches—just watching the river, relaxing, and dreaming about my future. I was amazed because it was so quiet and completely different from Bastrop. When I went up there, I felt like I was in another world.

I lived in Graniston Hall, a freshman dorm, that summer. And although my room was small—a cramped little space with a couple of desks and chairs and three beds—compared to my grandmother's house, it felt like a mansion. When my roommates arrived in the fall, things got a little tighter, but even with two other guys living there I still had far more space than I did when I lived with all my aunts and uncles at home.

That first summer, I worked from eight o'clock until five in the afternoon during the week. It was hard and it kept me busy. But it wasn't nearly as tough as picking or chopping cotton, and the grounds workers were given three meals a day. Usually, after I finished work and had dinner, I got together with the other athletes for pickup basketball and touch football games. In a way, it was what I had always imagined going off to camp would be. Although I missed my family and wrote to them once a week, that was one of the best summers I'd ever had.

School Begins

When the rest of the students arrived in the fall, things changed a lot. The campus came to life. Suddenly it was ringing with laughter, filled with kids rushing to classes and the dining halls. And for me, there was the challenge of facing up to something I had feared from the day I first attended Catholic school. I spent most of the summer alone, and I'd put off thinking about my stuttering. But when classes began, I knew I'd have to deal with it. And sure enough, there were problems. But almost from the first day, I found that college was a lot less difficult than high school.

The big difference was that in many of the courses I took, there was less class participation than I expected. Professors lectured, and we were expected to listen, take notes, and do the assigned readings. Question-and-answer sessions in the classroom were few and far between. When I found that grades would be determined mostly by papers and test scores, I breathed a huge sigh of relief. Standing up and talking in class had always been my greatest fear, and with that at a minimum, I was sure that I'd be all right at Southern. There were some little embarrassing moments when I was called on and had to fumble through an answer in class or read one of my own papers, but for the most part I glided through my college courses.

Campus Life

The biggest diversion I had when school opened was that the campus was filled with young women. Southern was a coed school with over five thousand students, about 60 percent of them female. I had never seen so many beautiful women in my life. Many of them were from Louisiana, so there were a lot of racially-mixed students (quadroons and octoroons). The campus was filled with light-skinned women who were often called "high yellows" or "light, bright, and damn near white," as well as hundreds of gorgeous brown- and dark-skinned women. After the term began, for the first week or so I walked around campus with my mouth hanging open. Being as shy as I was, I didn't say a whole lot to them. But for months, I felt like a little kid with his face pressed against a candy store window.

Like most black colleges, Southern had a lively social scene. There were parties every weekend, and although we didn't have fraternity houses, there were several active fraternities and sororities. Omega Phi Psi was the top fraternity, and all the guys on campus wanted to get into it. We also had chapters of the Kappas and the Alphas. The fraternity guys had the best parties and got most of the fine girls. Their parties were usually held at the home of one of the fraternity brothers who lived off campus, and nearly everybody tried to finagle an invitation—or, if they didn't get invited, crash the event.

Every so often, big-time stars like Odetta, Nancy Wilson, and B. B. King came in to perform at the gymnasium, and I went to all of the concerts. But I can't say that I was part of the college in-crowd. Outside of those concerts, I didn't get much involved in the social scene. In fact, I don't think I went to more than one party during freshman year, and I didn't stay very long that night. I felt uncomfortable the second I walked in there. It was partly my speech problem. I still had big trouble trying to talk to people I didn't know, and I was nervous about embarrassing myself in front of women. Then too, except for an occasional beer, I wasn't a drinker. And at those parties, if you didn't like booze and/or have a strong rap, you were always kind of an outsider.

Besides, like many black colleges at the time, there were some class and color barriers at Southern. Many light-skinned, middle-class students weren't too anxious to hang with dark-skinned kids from poorer families. Still, I don't recall any parties where the infamous paper bag test was used to bar students who weren't lighter than those beige bags. It seemed to me that the attitude came more from the parents than from the students. A lot of parents wanted to make sure their light-skinned sons and daughters met and married kids who were as light as or lighter than they. And since those parents influenced their kids, there was some color consciousness on campus and in the surrounding towns.

One of my buddies, a guy named James Gainor, ran dead into it. James was an outgoing, good-looking guy who was coal black. He thought of himself as a real lady killer, and he usually did have a fine coed on his arm. But when he hooked up with one of the real fair students at Southern, her parents and her friends starting giving them hell. James was determined, and I think he finally married the girl. But the problems he had were a tipoff to the value that a lot of bourgeois blacks placed on color and class even though we were right in the middle of the civil rights movement.

Since I didn't date much and wasn't much of partygoer (even later, after I'd become fairly well known as an All-Star basketball player on campus), I avoided most of those problems. I was basically a loner and kind of a gym rat. I went to classes and spent most of my free time in the gym. I was never a part of the campus social scene. I don't think I even had a real date until I was a junior.

Instead of joining one of the Greek fraternities like the Kappas or Alphas, I joined Alpha Phi Omega, a service fraternity that helped people in the community. We tried to assist folks with projects at their homes like building porches or repairing roofs; and, a little like Big Brothers today, we worked with young kids in the community to try to keep them off the street. It was an informal, loose-knit group, and we usually met in the room of one of the upperclassmen. Outside of sports, that was my only extracurricular activity.

61

freshman Year on the Basketball Team

Of course, getting ready for the basketball season was my main priority as a freshman. I had been practicing at least two or three hours a day since I arrived at school. And by the time workouts began in the fall, I was in excellent shape. I made the varsity that year and averaged 13 points a game competing against college competition that first season.

Southern University was in the Southwestern Atlantic Conference of the National Association of Intercollegiate Athletics (NAIA), a college sports organization that was founded in 1938 by a group of educators and promoters in Kansas. The founders included Dr. James Naismith, who invented the game of basketball. The aim of the NAIA was to promote the interests and achievements of small and moderate-size colleges, and they sponsored national tournaments in sports ranging from football to bowling. Initially, NAIA teams didn't get the media attention given to major schools in the National Collegiate Athletic Association (NCAA), and their tournament was never hyped like the NCAA's Final Four or the National Invitational Tournament (NIT). But by the 1960s, the NAIA was producing some fine basketball players. And small black schools like Tennessee State, which won the tournament three consecutive times from 1957 through 1959 when Dick Barnett and John Barnhill led the squad, were getting national attention. In fact, in 1964, the NAIA or "Little" All-American team produced more successful NBA players than the major college All-American squad.

Grambling, led by my old high school rival Willis Reed, won the NAIA championship in 1961, and during my first year at Southern, Zelmo Beaty, who went on to become a star center with the St. Louis Hawks, took Prairie View A&M to the championship. Both Grambling and Prairie View were on our schedule, and although we had a losing season, playing those top-notch teams helped improve my game. Along with Beaty, when they won the championship in 1962 Prairie View had Otis Taylor, who would later become an NFL superstar as a wide receiver. They had a reputation as rough, hard-nosed defensive players. Around the conference, teams would say, "Don't drive the lane on Prairie View, those guys will wipe you out."

But one of the things that our coach, Richard Mack, and his assistant, John Brown, had drilled into our heads was that you didn't let anyone intimidate you. In fact, Brown, a former football player, was one of the meanest, toughest guys I'd ever met; there was no way you could play for him if you were timid or scared. I learned not to fear anything on the basketball court. So when we played Prairie View, I drove to the hoop and scored the first time I got the ball. A few minutes later, I tried it again, and Beaty slammed me—knocked me up into the bleachers. I got up and made the foul shots. And the next time I got the ball, I went right back inside. I must have driven in there a dozen times that night. They hammered me every time, and we lost the game by 20 points. But after the buzzer, Beaty came over to me and said, "You're gonna be a good player, Love. Keep it up." I was sore as hell the next morning, but I had learned a lesson. By the end of that first season, I was confident that I could compete against the best college players.

Civil Unrest Hits Southern

Although most of my attention was focused on classwork and basketball that first year, there were a lot of other things happening on campus. Southern students had joined in the sit-in protests a few years earlier, and when I arrived in Scotlandsville, H. Rap Brown was enrolled at the school.

Brown was a local kid from Baton Rouge. Although he was only seventeen or eighteen years old when he was a sophomore, he had already built a reputation on campus. He loved to play basketball, and that's how I met him. He was also in a few of my classes, and we became friends during my first two years of college. He was about a year younger than I was, but you could see that he was determined to push ahead in the civil rights movement. He was already a leader in the campus student movement that became the Student National Coordinating Committee. What impressed me about him was his passion and intelligence. He could talk rings around most people on campus, including many of the professors, and he didn't let any slight pass without speaking out. He was constantly getting into rows with local authorities, teachers, the dean, the president. Brown was something else.

I didn't get involved in much of the protest activities on campus, but being a friend of Brown's, I heard about all of it. And once, in my sophomore year, I wound up right in the middle of things. In 1962, Southern students organized a protest march against state Jim Crow laws in Louisiana. I was one of about three thousand students who piled into buses and cars and gathered in front of the capitol building in Baton Rouge. The march had been announced in the press so the police were there with dogs and clubs when we arrived. They immediately told us to disperse and return to the campus. But nobody moved. It was chilly and drizzling rain that day, and we all huddled out there singing, "I Shall Not Be Moved" and "We Shall Overcome."

After two or three warnings, the police unleashed their dogs and started throwing tear gas canisters into the crowd. There was a stampede, and all hell broke loose. All of us started running away from the gas and dogs, and the police charged in with their clubs. A lot of people got hurt, trampled, or clubbed. Somehow, I got away unharmed. But five or six hundred students were arrested that day. Most of us had to hide out, then walk back to school.

Southern was closed for about a week after the demonstration, and a lot of students were expelled. Most had to leave school for a semester, and when they returned they had to go before the school disciplinary board before they could be reinstated. Southern's president, Felton G. Clark, took a lot of heat during that time. He was caught in a bind. When he refused to speak out against segregation, campus militants criticized him for not backing the students. But he had to walk a very thin line because he didn't want to offend the white patrons who supported the school financially.

The campus was in an uproar for months after that incident, and a lot of students just disappeared. I think that was when Brown left Southern. I don't remember seeing him afterward.

That was the only time I got involved in a mass protest or demonstration. The school administration was very conservative, and everybody knew that scholarship students were among the first to be expelled if there was any trouble.

During the remainder of my college career I concentrated on classes and playing basketball. I had decided to major in food and nutrition, and I had a lot of cooking courses. During the day, when I was in class, I often wore a kind of chef's uniform—white pants and a little white shirt. When my teammates saw me, they always laughed like hell. By then I was 6 feet 8 inches, and I guess I must have looked more than a little funny running around in that uniform. I didn't mind, though. Once I finished high school, I vowed that I'd never be hungry again. I wanted to make sure I had enough food, and since we got to eat everything we cooked, I couldn't wait to get to my cooking courses. A little laughter and teasing wasn't about to stop me from keeping my stomach full.

Sophomore Year on the Basketball Team

As a sophomore, I had a bust-out year in basketball. I averaged 23 points and 10 rebounds in my second year, and we finished with a winning record. I also made the Southwestern Athletic Conference (SWAC) All-Conference team and the NAIA All-American team for the first time that year.

I felt that I really came into my own during that season, and it seemed that my coaches felt the same way. I'll never forget the game we played in Pine Bluff, Arkansas, against Arkansas A&M. In the fourth quarter, we were losing by 7 points when Coach Mack called a timeout and told the team, "Look, we can win this game. Just pass the ball to Love." The next twelve times down the court, they got the ball to me and everybody cleared out. Even though I was double- and triple-teamed, I hit all twelve shots. I drove, posted up, and hit jumpers from the outside—I was in a zone that night. I couldn't miss, and we came

65

back to win the game. I didn't know about it until later, but I heard that after that night, the coaches started calling me "the Lord's prayer."

Junior Year on the Basketball Team

The following year, as a junior I averaged 25 points and 15 rebounds. Again, I was selected to the All-Conference and NAIA All-American teams. We finished with a 15–11 record, and after the season ended there was talk about Southern having a good shot at winning the conference title next year.

That spring, I was also notified that I was one of twenty-four players from small colleges selected to practice for the 1964 Olympic Trials. We joined twenty-four guys from the major NCAA schools and began practicing at Rockhurst College in Kansas City. The best college basketball players in America were invited to those trials. At first, the guys from small schools competed against each other, and players from the larger colleges had their own workouts. Then the two squads were cut to fifteen players each, and they went out on separate tours.

I made the first cut, and while I was on tour we played against the Russian national team in Peoria, Kansas. We had a terrific team that was led by Willis Reed and Lucious Jackson, and the tryout and tour were probably the most challenging experiences I had in college basketball. I didn't make the next cut to twelve players, so I never had the chance to work out with the major college stars like Dave Stallworth, Walt Hazzard, Billy Cunningham, and Bill Bradley.

Finally, Lucious Jackson and Willis Reed were the only two small-college players to make the Olympic team. Still, my experience that spring gave me all of the confidence in the world that I could play on the next level. I began feeling that it didn't matter what school one went to or how big it was—it was just a matter of who could put the ball in the hole. When I returned to Southern after the Olympic Trials, I was convinced I could play with anybody.

A Different Baba

That summer, I went back to Bastrop for a few days, then went to Los Angeles to see my mother and stepfather for the first time since they'd moved. They owned a small grocery store in Watts, and my mom had been sending me little boxes of toiletries, canned foods, and snacks every so often. She even included a few dollars in the package when she could. When I got out there, I was a little anxious about seeing Baba. We hadn't said more than a word or two to each other since the gym shoe incident. It was a little awkward at first, but after a few days we began to hit it off.

It seemed to me that he had changed. For one thing, he'd become a devout Christian and he didn't seem as mean and irritable as I remembered him. He had always been a sports fan, so when he read about the Olympic Trials and my success at Southern I guess his opinion of me also changed. He was surprised that I was doing so well, and I also think he was proud of me. We talked a lot while I was out there, but we didn't discuss the bad times in Bastrop.

There was no doubt that the way he treated me and his own kids had left some scars on the family. Even while I was out there, I could see that nobody really showed any affection around the house. After years of tension and having to walk into a room with your jaw all tight because you were on guard, it was hard to be an open, loving person. Years later, when I talked to my half brothers and sisters about it, it seemed that everybody was in denial. I realized that a lot of his hostility toward me came up because I was another man's child. But Baba had also been rough on his own children. They couldn't dance or listen to music in his house, and they couldn't go to the movies. My sister Dorothy had run away from home when he tried to beat her after she came in late one night. She never came back and later we found out she was pregnant. But when we talked about it, they all claimed that it wasn't that bad. "Nothing happened," they insisted. "That's the way he was raised. He didn't know any other way to act."

I hadn't forgotten the way he treated me, and I knew I never would. But by the time I saw Baba in Los Angeles, it was only a memory. I didn't hold a grudge, and I didn't want to dwell on it. Baba had become a real fan of mine, and although it didn't erase the way he treated me as a child, I left feeling that we had gotten rid of some of the bad blood. After that trip, I was never reluctant about visiting my mother's home.

Senior Year on the Basketball Team

My final year of college was my best. That season, Rick Barry was the nation's leading scorer with a 37-point average, but I was right there in the top five with 31 points per game. I also averaged 18 rebounds and had the third-best field goal percentage in the conference. More important, Southern won the SWAC championship, and for the first time during my college career our little school was invited to the NAIA tournament in Kansas City. I made the All-Tournament team, but we lost to Ouachita Baptist University, a team out of Arkadelphia, Arkansas, in the quarterfinals. Still, I was proud of that team and the guys on it. During my four years of college, Southern had gone from a mediocre team with a losing record to conference champs and the NAIA tournament. It was a tremendous group achievement, and I felt that I was ready to move on to the pros.

I knew that a few NBA scouts had been following our team since my junior year, and when I was a senior there were one or two in the stands for most games. But when I was invited to San Francisco to try out for the United States national basketball team at the end of the 1965 season, I knew that every NBA team would be watching. I made the cut and went on to play in a seven-game series against the Russian team. The United States team had some of the best college players from the NAIA and NCAA, including Nate Bowman and Dave Stallworth of Wichita State University, Gail Goodrich of UCLA, and Flynn Robinson of

Wyoming University. We played the Russians in St. Louis, Las Vegas, Indianapolis, Los Angeles, and San Francisco, and all of the games were well publicized. During that series, I started getting some of the national exposure that I'd missed playing at a small black college.

All during the spring, I was on pins and needles waiting to hear who had been chosen in the NBA draft. I was anxious, but I truly felt that I was one of the best basketball players at the college level. I had been a three-time All-SWAC and NAIA All-American selection. I was the all-time leading scorer at Southern. And I was the first black player to make the All-South team, which included NCAA and NAIA players. Rick Barry from the University of Miami, Fred Hetzel from Davidson, and Billy Cunningham from North Carolina were also selected. Making the All-South team was my crowning achievement in college basketball.

At that time, I could run like a deer, run all day, and never get tired. For four years, all I'd done in the summertime was train, play basketball, and work. I never smoked—did very little drinking, just an occasional beer at that time. I was in tip-top shape. I just hoped that the scouts recognized that I was as ready as I knew I was.

Ready for the Future

I'd done just about everything I'd hoped for in basketball, but the most important thing that happened to me during my college years was meeting Betty Elizabeth Smith. I met her in my junior year when Robert Smith, a classmate who was also from Bastrop, introduced us. Robert had seen these two tall girls on campus and struck up a conversation. He told Betty that he could introduce her to the star of the basketball team if she was interested. A few weeks later, I picked her up at her house, and we went out on a date. We hit it off right away, and after that evening, we saw each other constantly.

We were married during my senior year. When I graduated from Southern with a degree in food and nutrition, I'd not only had a very successful basketball career but I was also married to one of the most beautiful women I'd ever met and I was looking forward to becoming a father. Later in 1965, we had our first child, Kevin. I was on top of the world.

6

BREAKING INTO THE NBA

There I was with the guys I'd dreamed about,
read about in magazines, and followed on the
radio since I was a teenager. Now I was part
of their team.

W HEN I HEARD THAT I'D BEEN selected by the Cincinnati
Royals in the fourth round of the 1965 NBA draft, I almost
passed out. I had known I had a shot, but for Betty and me
it was a godsend. We were just starting our family, and we
knew that the chance for a career in professional basketball
would give us an opportunity to start things off on the right
foot. For me, it was even more thrilling. It was the realization
of the dream I'd had since I was a child, and there's nothing like
seeing your dream materialize right before your eyes.

Rookie Camp and My First Contract

That summer, when I arrived in Cincinnati for rookie camp, I
quickly discovered that being drafted was just the first step.
Making the team would be a lot tougher. In 1965 there were
only nine teams in the entire league, and each team drafted
scores of players. We were competing against each other to fill
a handful of openings in a league that only employed 108 players. It was a dog-eat-dog situation. Being drafted was no assur-
ance that you would even get close to playing for a professional
team, and everybody who showed up at camp knew it.

On top of that, we were trying out for one of the league's premier teams. The franchise later changed its name to the Kings and moved to Kansas City, then to Sacramento. But in the mid-'60s, Cincinnati had one of the NBA's elite teams. They never won a championship, but with stars like Jerry Lucas, Adrian Smith, and Oscar Robertson, they drew fairly large crowds and were always competitive. All the rookies knew that cracking their lineup would not be easy.

That summer, it seemed as though there were a thousand guys trying out for the team at Cincinnati Gardens, the Royals' home arena. They had players from all over the country, big-time college players like Walt Wesley, Nate Bowman, and Flynn Robinson, and a lot of small-college guys like me. They divided us into teams, and for weeks we played scrimmage games. It was tough, cutthroat basketball, because everybody knew that if your team lost more than once you wouldn't get a chance to play again. That's how they trimmed down the squad. Guys were hacking, elbowing—anything to show how rough they were and how much they wanted to make it. There were scuffles and face-offs everyday. I was lucky enough to play for a good team, and we won all of our rookie scrimmages.

I had a terrific rookie camp, averaging nearly 20 points a game. And when it was all over, the general manager, Pepper Wilson, called me into his office. "Bob," he said, "we really like what we've seen in camp. We think you're going to make this team." Then he showed me a contract. The salary was $8,000. More money than I'd ever thought about making. He also placed several stacks of bills on his desk, each one a little bigger than the other. My eyes swelled up as big as apples when he pointed at one of the smaller stacks next to the contract and said, "Bob, if you sign with us, this is all yours."

72   I stared at that stack of money, and all I saw on top were twenty-dollar bills. Now, I had never even seen a hundred dollars in my lifetime. I couldn't see what was beneath the twenties, but I didn't hesitate for more than a minute before I looked up and said, "I'll sign."

I signed right there, and he pushed the stack of bills over to me. "This is your bonus, son," he said. "Enjoy it." It was a wad, and when I walked out of his office, my pocket looked like it had the mumps.

I went straight to the airport and got on a Delta prop plane headed for Louisiana. I counted that money over and over, all the way back to Baton Rouge. There were several twenties, a few tens and fives, and a whole bunch of ones. Altogether, it was about two hundred dollars. I had never seen that much money in my life. Back in Baton Rouge, I must have partied with Betty and my friends for two weeks.

My First Stint in the NBA

That fall, I went back to Cincinnati to report to the Royals' training camp. Only a couple of rookies were invited, most of them from major colleges, but all the veterans were there. I knew that this was going to be my big test, the real deal as we used to say. I was surrounded by great players: Jerry Lucas, Walt Wesley, Adrian Smith, Tom Hawkins, Happy Hairston, Flynn Robinson, Nate Bowman, and, of course, the Big O, Oscar Robertson. Just being out there with those guys made me nervous as hell but still I had a lot of confidence in my own game. I stuck with the team throughout the exhibition season, and it was an amazing experience. Finally, I had a chance to compete with all those players I'd dreamed about in my own backyard.

I'll never forget the first time I played against Bill Russell. It was an exhibition game in Boston, and before the game our coach, Jack McMahon, warned the new guys to watch out for Russell because he was the best shot blocker in the league. But, being a rookie, I wasn't impressed. Hey, I was naive and fearless. I thought I could jump out of the gym, that nobody could block my shots.

Near the end of the first quarter, McMahon put me into the game, and a few minutes later we stole the ball from Boston. Oscar Robertson and I ran out on the fast break. When I got the pass from Oscar, Russell was the only guy between me and the basket. I palmed the ball and faked a behind-the-back pass to Oscar. When Russell went for the feint, I kept the ball and went in for the dunk. The crowd went wild. They had never seen a dunk quite like that before.

At first, I couldn't believe that I'd done it. It was just as if I was back in Bastrop in my neighbor's backyard. It happened exactly the way I'd dreamed about it. But the thrill didn't last that long. As we ran back down the court, Russell caught up with me and grabbed my arm. "Rookie," he said, "listen here. Do you know who I am?"

I was stuttering, so I said, "Y-y-yes sir, you're B-Bi-Bill Russell."

"Let me tell you something, boy," he said. "Don't you ever bring your ass in here and try that shot again. Matter of fact, don't even think about it. Don't even dream that you ever thought about dunking on me again."

"Ah-all right, Mr. Ru-Russell," I stuttered.

Then, just before the quarter ended, Oscar and I broke away from the pack again. This time, when Oscar gave me the ball, he was smiling, and he yelled, "Go get 'em, Bean. Go get 'em." I guess I was a little overconfident, so I made the mistake of trying the same fake. Russell was waiting for it. He slapped the ball out of my hand, and it bounced off my head and flew out of bounds. I went sprawling right along with the ball. When I got up, Russell said, "I don't think you heard me, rookie. The lane belongs to me. I don't ever want to see you in here trying to dunk again!"

That was the last time I tried a slam on Bill Russell. And for weeks the guys teased me about it.

Still, I did very well during the exhibition season, and I really thought I had the team made. But just one week before the season started, the coach called me into his office. "Bob, I'm

74

sorry," he said. "I just don't have room for you this year. You were terrific for a rookie, but we can only carry twelve guys. Besides, I think you need a little more weight to compete under the basket with NBA players. That doesn't mean we're not interested, though. If you're willing, I'd like you to play for the Trenton Colonials in the Eastern League this year."

Down to the Minors

In the '60s, the Eastern League, which is now known as the Continental Basketball Association, was the training ground, or minor leagues, for the NBA. If a team thought a player had potential and might help them in the future, they would arrange to have him play for a season to sharpen his game. The Eastern League's rosters were filled with guys who just missed the cut in the NBA, former NBA players, and a lot of other guys who were hoping to catch the eye of NBA scouts. I still thought I should have made the Royals that year, and I was disappointed; but in November of 1965, I went to Trenton, got a room at the local YMCA, and began playing for the Colonials.

We played on weekends, and they only paid us fifty dollars a game. There was no way I could support a family on that, so the Colonials owners also got me a job as a dietitian intern at Ancora Mental Hospital during the week. Later that season, I worked for the New Jersey State Hospital for Children in Woodbridge. Although I was convinced that the Royals would call me back, I was glad to get some experience in the field I'd studied in college. Players didn't have agents in the '60s and team owners could do just about anything they wanted to do, and I was just beginning to learn that professional athletics wasn't the best-paying or most secure profession that a person could choose.

75

See, after I returned to the Royals' training camp in the fall, I discovered that I didn't have a no-cut contract. I'd been so excited at being signed that I didn't look at the small print.

Once they released me, Cincinnati didn't owe me a dime. The only guys who got no-cut deals were the number-one or number-two draft choices. As a fourth-round choice from Southern University, a small black college, I was not very high in the pecking order. There was room for only an elite few players in the NBA, and there were a lot of talented ballplayers around. Most of those openings went to athletes from well-known schools with big-time basketball programs.

Race and Privilege in the 1960s NBA

Although things had begun to change during the mid-'60s, there were still a lot of quotas, segregation, and stereotyped judgments about basketball players at the college and pro level. At the big-time colleges, coaches seemed afraid to play more than a couple of black players at the same time. Talent aside, there was concern about the reaction of alumni and fans to teams with more blacks than whites. Nobody said that, of course. The argument was that every team had to have one or two white players to give it the needed "balance" and "discipline." Some coaches, like Adolph Rupp at the University of Kentucky, refused to suit up any blacks. A lot of the old assumptions about the capabilities of black athletes were shattered when Texas Western, which started five black players, beat Rupp's number-one ranked, all-white Kentucky team in the NCAA championship game in 1966 while I was playing for Trenton in the Eastern League.

NBA coaches shared some of the same attitudes at the time. And in the mid-'60s, a lot of attention was paid to how many black players each team had. One of the results was that a lot of teams were reluctant to consider players from small black colleges in the South, and only a few had made the NBA. The most successful were John Barnhill, Ben Warley, and Dick "Skull" Barnett from Tennessee State, Zelmo Beaty from Prairie View A&M, Willis Reed from Grambling, and my old high school teammate Lucious Jackson, who went to Texas Southern before transferring to Pan American University. It was a different ballgame back then. There were a limited number of black players in the NBA. I got the chance to play basketball that year, but I had to have a second job to support myself.

Playing with the Colonials

During my stint with the Trenton Colonials, I really began to appreciate the advice of John Brown, Southern's assistant coach. It was competitive, roughhouse ball, and if you could be intimidated, had any fear, you didn't stand a chance. There was a fight almost every game. Still, some great playground players came through that league. I played with Walter Dukes while I was there. He couldn't shoot very well, but he was rough—a great defensive player and rebounder. Tom Stith, the All-American from St. Bonaventure, was also in the league. He was only 6 feet 5 inches, but he could rebound, shoot with either hand, and float to the basket as well as anyone around. Si Green, the former Duquesne All-American who had played for five different NBA teams, could leap over the basket. Al Butler was a pure shooting guard from Niagara who had been released by the Bullets; he was an excellent defensive player and could run an offense like clockwork. And there were some terrific ballplayers most NBA fans never saw. One of the best I faced in that league was Wally Choice. Wally was a forward who could flat-out play. He had a lot of talent, but he never caught the attention of the scouts. In those days you had to find the right team and the right situation, and they had to have a spot available for you.

If nothing else, playing in the Eastern League toughened me up. It was a battle every night, because just like me, every player out there was trying to prove he could play in the NBA. I averaged over 22 points and 15 rebounds. All in all, I had a great year, and the Colonials battled for the Eastern Division title up until the last few games of the season. Finally, the Wilmington Blue Bombers beat us out and went on to win the championship. I stayed in New Jersey working and playing basketball until the spring, then returned to Louisiana to see my family in Bastrop, and my son and my wife Betty, who were staying in Baton Rouge.

Back to the NBA

When I went back to the Royals' training camp in 1966, I made the team. It was what I'd dreamed about all my life, but after they told me I'd survived the cut, I still couldn't believe it. When I walked into the locker room to get dressed for the first practice with the other eleven guys, I was floating on air. There I was with the guys I'd dreamed about, read about in magazines, and followed on the radio since I was a teenager. Now I was part of their team. Being in the same room with them—Oscar Robertson, Jerry Lucas, Adrian Smith, and the others—I was in awe. It took a while to get over that feeling, and even after the season started, I still had a hard time accepting the idea that I even knew those guys, let alone that I was playing on the same floor, the same team with them.

My Friend the Legend

Of course, Oscar was my favorite. He was already a legend, and everybody on that team looked up to him. He and I had gotten to know each other the year before, and during the 1966–67 season we got to be really good friends. I was just a rookie out of Louisiana, and I hadn't traveled much, spent much time in big cities, or eaten in fine restaurants with exotic menus and drinks. I think Oscar realized that I was a big old country boy who had never really been anywhere, and he just took me under his wing.

After I made the team, the other players kind of took to my nickname, Butterbeans. Then Oscar started calling me Bayou Bean or just B. He was the team leader, and everybody fol-

78

lowed his lead, so that name stuck. During the time I played for the Royals, that's what the rest of the guys called me.

Oscar guided me through training camp in my rookie year. My number was 12 then, and Oscar's was 14, so my locker was right next to his. And when we traveled for exhibition games, he chose me as his first roommate. We spent a lot of time together, and he was constantly tutoring me, giving me little tips, going over the things that he said separated average ballplayers from the great ones. I was just plain lucky to be on the same team with him as a rookie.

No One Like Him

Oscar came into the game knowing how to shoot, pass, and rebound. He is the only guy ever to average a triple double for the entire season. Magic Johnson is the only guy who ever came close to it, but I don't think anybody will ever match that record. He is right up there with the five or six best players to ever play the game. He was 6 feet 5 inches, 220 pounds, so the small guys couldn't guard him, and he was quick enough to go around the big guys. He was unstoppable.

During the years I played, I got to know Wilt Chamberlain, and I always considered him the most dominant player ever because of his height, his scoring and shot-blocking ability, and his rebounding. Bill Russell was probably the most determined player I faced. He had a meanness and desire to win that was unbelievable, and nobody won more championships than he did.

Michael Jordan had that meanness, that take-no-prisoners attitude. He had that head game along with all the physical talent of a Baylor or Robertson. Watching him play was like listening to great music. He was beautiful. And as far as winning, taking over games, and creating excitement, nobody matched Michael. He was one of the greatest, if not *the* greatest. None of the guys before him came close to his performance during the

1997–98 season. At age thirty-five, he led the league in scoring; was MVP of the season, the All-Star Game, and the play-offs; and won the championship. He did it all, and no one can dispute that. Still, Oscar had a better understanding of the game than anyone I've ever seen. He didn't have Michael's killer instinct and wasn't as flamboyant, but he was probably the most fundamentally sound player to ever play in the NBA.

Oscar the Coach

During practices, he would pull me aside and share as much as he could with me. He made me practice defense by guarding him in one-on-one games. I always guarded him in practice, and every time he went past me or faked, and I went up to block his shot, he stopped and took the time to tell me what I'd done wrong. We'd go over to the side, and he'd say, "Now B, you can't go for that kind of fake, you got to stay on your feet and stop me from getting by you. You gotta be tough."

I learned more about basketball in those practice sessions than any coach has ever taught me. And pretty soon I began to respect the defensive side of the game. Although I was never that successful against Oscar, I started to take pride in stopping my opponent. I was becoming a tenacious defensive player.

I also improved my shot during those sessions. Oscar would always tell me, "Butter, if a player is a foot or more away from you, he shouldn't be able to block your shot. See, the offensive man always has the advantage. The guy guarding you doesn't know if you're going to drive or shoot. He's always guessing. And if you can drive *and* shoot the jumper, he can't stop you. When the ball is in your hands, you have to be a threat to do both those things."

We practiced nearly every day. He'd have me stand on a chair so that I towered over him. I held my hands up as high as possible, and when he stood one foot away from me, I still couldn't block his shot. Even when I jumped as high as I could, I couldn't touch the shot. He just waited until I was on my way

Making the NBA with
the Cincinnati Royals
in 1966 was what I
had dreamed about
all my life.
© *The Sporting News*

With my mother, Lula Bell Hunter Cleveland.
Courtesy of Bob Love

Going up for a jump shot against
Portland at Chicago Stadium in 1972.
© *Corbis/Bettmann—*UPI

No one had a bigger impact on my
childhood than my grandmother, Ella
Mae Hunter. She gave me the strength
to face the challenges I've encountered
and taught me never to quit.
Courtesy of Bob Love

The Bulls teams I played on were hard-nosed and fought hard on defense.

© AP/Wide World Photos

Facing two of our Western
Conference rivals, the
Warriors (top) and Lakers.
The Bulls reached the
conference finals in 1975,
only to lose to the Warriors
in a tough seven game series.
Top photo © Corbis/Bettmann—UPI
Bottom photo © Sports Illustrated

Looking to make something happen against Los Angeles.
© *Sports Illustrated*

On January 25, 1974, I scored my 10,000th career point during a game against Seattle. Referee Don Murphy presented me with the game ball.
© *AP/Wide World Photos*

Boxing out Boston's Paul Silas during the 1974–75 season.
© *Neil Liefer/Sports Illustrated*

I'm holding back
my emotions as the
Bulls retire #10.
© *John Swart/*AP *Photo*

Receiving a commemorative ring from Bulls vice president Jerry
Krause on January 14, 1994, the night my jersey was retired at
Chicago Stadium.
© *John Swart/*AP *Photo*

I'm proud that I have become an effective communicator.
© *Courtesy of the Chicago Bulls*

down. Finally, I got it. It was all about timing and keeping that one-foot distance from the defender. If he got closer, you had to go around him, but if he gave you that little bit of room, you could always get the shot off. You didn't have to hurry or over-power anybody. It was finesse. You just had to recognize the instant when the defender was coming down and release the ball at exactly the right time. If I got the shot off right at that split-second, it was almost impossible for anybody to block it.

During my eleven and a half years in the league, I don't think I had my jump shot blocked more than a dozen times. I always remembered what Oscar had taught me. I always held the ball up high in the shooting position. And if the defender didn't jump, I was able to shoot in one quick motion. Nobody got it. In all those years, nobody understood how I got that shot off. I credit that to Oscar.

At 6 feet 5 inches, Oscar was also a great rebounder, one of the few guards to ever average more than 10 rebounds a game. And one of the things he drilled into my head was to keep the ball up high when I grabbed it, never bringing it down or bouncing it before I was sure the defense had cleared. Nowa-days, nearly every time a big man gets a rebound, he drops it down or tries to bounce it. Oscar taught me to think of the bas-ketball as a piece of cheese and look at all those little guards as if they were rats: if you dropped the cheese, all those rats were gonna come after it, and a lot of times they were going to get it.

A Lot to Learn

I learned so much from him that I can't even begin to give him all the credit he deserves. And we had some great times hang-ing out with the other guys. We practiced at the campus gym of the University of Miami, which was in Oxford, Ohio, and every night after practice all the guys would go into town to this little college bar. We'd sit around and tell jokes. Jerry Lucas was a great storyteller, and he would usually get things started. He could keep you in knots for days. Then Oscar or another guy would tell a joke. Oscar and Jerry liked teasing me, and sooner or later one of them would say, "OK, Butter, it's your turn." The laughter started the moment they said it.

Still, I'd fumble around and try to start a story. Of course, I was stammering and stuttering, out of breath. Most times, right in the middle of my story, Oscar would stand up. "Bayou, I'm going to the bathroom," he'd say. "But don't stop. I'll be back in time for the punch line." Everybody would crack up, but I didn't really mind. I loved being with those guys, and I knew they didn't mean any harm.

We had some great times during training camp, and as time for the season opener approached, I was beginning to feel more confident about my game. I thought I was ready to get started, and I couldn't wait for the real season to begin. It didn't take long for me to discover that I still had a lot to learn—both on and off the court.

7

ROOKIE YEAR WITH THE ROYALS

*There is a special feeling about being a pro
athlete that's hard to describe.*

I DIDN'T GET MANY MINUTES at the start of the 1966–67 season.
I was the ninth or tenth man, and the coach would slip me in
near the end of games when we were way ahead or way behind.
At first, I didn't mind. I was young, and I knew I had a lot to
learn. I considered myself lucky just to be sitting on the bench.
There is a special feeling about being a pro athlete that's hard to
describe. You can't help swelling up with pride when you realize
that you're one of a very select group being paid to do something
that you absolutely love. That group had expanded with Chicago's return to the league that year, but there were still only ten
teams and 120 guys in the league. I kept telling myself that I was
fortunate just suiting up with them.

Still, I came to every game excited and ready to play. I was
convinced that I could excel against those guys, and every time
I stepped onto the court I put everything I had into it. Although
playing in front of the home crowd at Cincinnati Gardens was
exciting, I was even more pumped up when we went on the road.

Road Rules

I loved traveling with the team. Rooming with Oscar was like
going to school. And throughout my rookie season, I felt like a
little boy sitting at the knee of an old master. I tried to remember every word he said. But the travel itself was also a thrill for

me. See, when I was growing up down south, we couldn't even afford to travel out of state. And although I'd been to a few large cities when I was traveling with my college team and with the United States national team, I was never allowed to be on my own. We were closely watched and spent most of the time in hotels or the arenas. I'd been to New York, Los Angeles, and a few other places, but Kansas City, New Orleans, and Baton Rouge were the only big towns that I'd ever really seen and had a chance to get to know. When the Royals went to places like Chicago, New York, Los Angeles, and San Francisco, giving me the chance to really see those cities, my eyes lit up like lightbulbs.

In those days, they made it real hard on us rookies. It felt like being hazed by a college fraternity. We had to take care of all the little annoying things like carrying the other players' bags or running out in the rain or snow to get a taxi when we left a restaurant. And we were always getting ragged by the veterans. On flights, while the stars—Oscar and maybe Jerry—sat in first-class, I rode coach with all the rest of the team. I could barely fit into those tight little seats; my knees would be pressed all up against my chest and believe me it wasn't comfortable. But I was so excited about being a pro that I didn't mind. I was as happy as a kid at the circus.

Teams didn't throw money around like they do today, so we couldn't afford to live that high on the hog. They gave us maybe eight dollars a day for meals. Some guys were either so tight or so strapped for cash that they saved the money and took it back home. Maybe I was still thinking about the old days when my pockets were always empty, but it seemed like a lot to me. I'd spend every cent, buying junk food like hot dogs, hamburgers, french fries, and pop.

84 Even Oscar got more excited when we went to play the New York Knicks or elite teams like the Boston Celtics with Russell or the Philadelphia 76ers with Wilt. He was particularly fond of playing in New York because of the media. "If you play well in New York," he always said, "you've got it made. Everybody will hear about it."

The Magic of New York

The first time we went to New York, he said, "All right, Bayou, we're going to the Big Apple. You hang with me. I'll show you the ropes." Watching him play on those trips was one of the highlights of my rookie season. Oscar raised his game two or three levels when he played in the Garden. He always put on a show. Nobody stopped him. We lost a few games there, but he always rose to the occasion.

He nearly always had a triple double—30 or 40 points, 10 to 15 rebounds, and more than a dozen assists. Oscar loved going to New York and lighting them up. He was at his best against the top teams. And after the games the press would always mob him. He'd sit there answering questions, sometimes for an hour or so, and since I was his roommate I'd stand at the door with my gym bag waiting for him.

We played at the old Garden on Forty-ninth Street and Eighth Avenue in my rookie year, and we stayed at Loew's Motor Inn. When we left the Garden, Oscar and I would always drop our bags off at the hotel. Then we'd take a walk. I was so happy to be in New York with him; I followed him around like a little puppy. He was a superstar, and when people recognized him on the street they'd shout, "That's the Big O," and run up to ask for an autograph. Cars and taxis stopped and blew their horns. Sooner or later, we'd pass a liquor store, and Oscar would say, "Let's stop in here." He usually bought a bottle of Early Times. I'd get a pop or bottle of beer—that Early Times was a monster. We were always tired after a game, so instead of going out to eat, we usually went back to the hotel. Oscar liked to relax and unwind in his own room, where he wouldn't have to deal with any more fans.

Skull Sessions

We either picked up food from a restaurant and took it back to the room or ordered from room service. Oscar loved cheeseburgers, and most times he'd order a couple of burgers and some fries. I'd have the same thing. I figured I couldn't go wrong if I followed his lead. Then we'd sit there, and he would go over the game with me. He was amazing. He analyzed everything that happened on the court. It seemed as though he could remember every shot, every pass and cut, every rebound or foul. Oscar was a perfectionist.

"If you want to score in the NBA, you've got to move without the ball," he kept telling me. "The guys who move will always get their shots. You have to stay focused, see the whole court, and move if you want to play in this league."

It took some time before I understood it, but besides his incredible talent, one of the secrets to Oscar's success was that he was constantly in motion when he played. It didn't look like he was exerting himself, but if you looked closely you could see that he never stopped. He had it down to a science. There were some very good players on our team that year, but none of us could really match his ability. In fact, there were very few guys in the league who equaled his performance on a regular basis. And like many truly great players, he didn't have much patience with guys who didn't understand the game as well as he did or couldn't do the things he did. On the court, he had a short fuse.

He couldn't stand silly mistakes or lack of concentration. Although he was upset when someone missed an easy, open shot on a break, he'd accept it if it didn't happen too often. He would even come over and encourage you. But if you muffed a pass, didn't run the lane on a fast break, didn't get to the right position on the court in a set play, or had some mental lapse, he would ignore you the next time down the court. You wouldn't see the ball. Oscar always ran the offense, and he would make sure you didn't get it. He had a look that could kill, and if you missed a layup or an open jump shot, he'd glare at you until you wanted to take yourself out of the game. He was one of the most intense, competitive athletes I ever saw, and he expected everybody else to play the same way. When I started in the NBA, he was the player who kept the competitive fire burning inside me.

During those talks in our rooms after road games—he called them "skull sessions"—he went over the strengths and weaknesses of the opposing players. "Cazzie Russell, you got to get up in his face, force him to his left," he'd say. Or he'd remind me to force left-handed players like Lenny Wilkens to their right. "Make him go right, Bayou. Don't let him trick you. That's his weakness." Or, when we had played Boston, he'd say, "John Havlicek is great from the outside. You have to play him tight, make him drive, Bayou. You can't stop him defensively, but on offense you can take him inside and post him up. Make him work. I'll get you the ball."

Then he'd point out the times when Jerry Lucas or Happy Hairston or I didn't cut to the hoop when we should have, or fumbled a pass that should have led to a basket. He insisted that you had to have a fluid offense if you wanted to win, and nothing made him madder than players who just stood around—didn't move without the ball. He was always on their case. But he was just as hard on himself. He'd remember a twelve-foot jumper that he missed and say, "Damn, how did I miss that chippie, I had him in the air. I should have knocked it down." Or, "You know, when Willis came over to double-team in the second quarter, I should have made that pass. I blew it. But you had the right idea. Keep moving to the hoop, next time I'll get it to you."

Oscar was intense, but when he was away from the game and just hanging out, he was altogether different. Once, in 1967, during my second year in Cincinnati, the Royals drafted Bill Dinwiddie. He was from Muncie, a small city in Indiana. He had a lot of ability, and he stuck with the team. But Bill was a lot like I was when I came up. He was from the country, and he didn't dress well. Oscar had a closet full of clothes, so he gave Bill a suit and a couple of sport coats, then took him downtown and bought him some accessories. He was like that, had a heart as big as his game.

The press made a big thing of it, but I wasn't surprised when Oscar gave up one of his kidneys to save his daughter's life in 1998. He was the most generous, giving person I met during

87

my NBA career. And once you became his friend, you were a friend for life.

Bayou in the Big City

Traveling with the Royals, seeing new places, and hanging out with my teammates were among my fondest memories of that first year. And since I was probably one of the greenest rookies ever to come up to the NBA, particularly off the court, I had a lot to learn. I was always doing or saying something that cracked the team up.

Most of the time, it started because I was so naive. I remember once during that first year when we were waiting to catch a plane on our way back from New York. We were sitting in the cocktail lounge playing cards, and the waitress came around and asked what we wanted to order. I wasn't a big drinker but I wanted to impress the guys, so I listened to what they ordered.

"I'll take an Early Times and Coke," Oscar said.

"Give me a Manhattan," Jerry Lucas said.

I think Happy Hairston asked for a beer, someone asked for a Seagram's and 7-Up, and another player ordered a Scotch and soda. Then the waitress turned to me and said, "Sir, what would you like?" I didn't know what to order, but after hearing the names of all those fancy mixed drinks, I didn't want to seem too country. I wanted to fit in.

I looked at the list of drinks on the back of the menu, and since we were just leaving New York and Manhattan, the name of one drink jumped out at me. I looked up, smiled, and, trying to sound as cosmopolitan as I could, said, "I'll take ah-a M-ma-man-hattan and 7-Up." Jerry started laughing so hard that he dropped his cards. Then everybody at the table busted out laughing. Even then, I just sat there smiling. I didn't know why it was so funny, and nobody explained until we got on the plane. They teased me about that for the rest of the year.

Gaining Time

As the season went on, I began getting a little more game time. I was a forward, so I played behind Len Chappell, Jerry Lucas, and Happy Hairston. Hairston was truly a terrific offensive rebounder. He was very active on the boards, and if you didn't block him out all day he'd kill you. He was also a pretty good defensive player. But he didn't have an outside jump shot, and some guys didn't like his attitude. See, a lot of times when Hairston was slated to guard one of the league's top-scoring forwards, he'd show up at the arena not feeling his best. That didn't go over well with some players, and of course the coach wasn't too pleased. Although Hairston averaged 17 points a game the next year, he was traded to Detroit in the middle of the season. I was never sure what was going through Hairston's mind or what was really bothering him, but I wasn't that concerned. I did know that whenever he couldn't play, I got more time on the court. And I was anxious to prove myself.

About halfway through the season, I began getting the chance to play bigger minutes. It was primarily because of my defense. They would match me up with the opponent's top forward or, sometimes, the top guard. Coach McMahon didn't like to have Oscar defend our opponent's highest-scoring guard, since he was in total control of our offense. They didn't use the term *two guard* at the time, but he was a combination point guard and scoring guard. He brought the ball up the court and ran the offense. He led the team in assists, but he was also the scoring leader and one of our best rebounders. Oscar could play defense with the best, but the Royals couldn't afford to have him work hard at both ends of the court. That's how I initially got my shot.

When I wasn't matched against a forward I could play the big guards, and I was fast enough to cover most of the smaller guards. And since I knew it was one way that I could carve out a niche on the team, I began concentrating on defense. It was a challenge, and I jumped at the opportunity to prove myself. My most rewarding experiences as a rookie came when I guarded guys like Dave Bing, who was a rookie with Detroit; Rick Barry, a second-year man with San Francisco; or Elgin Baylor and Jerry West, who had teamed up in Los Angeles.

Most of the time, I didn't get a lot of minutes on the court, but I appeared in over sixty games that year. I only averaged 6 points a game, but by the end of the year the coach was playing me more for my defensive contribution.

Set Back by Injury

In one of the last games of the season, I went in for a dunk against Philadelphia, and one of their guards ran under my legs. I came down hard on my back. I was so anxious to play that I stayed in the game for a few more minutes, but the instant it happened I thought something was wrong. I didn't find out how serious it was until after the game.

When the buzzer sounded and we went to the locker room, my left leg started to throb and ache, and then it went numb. A few minutes later, I began feeling dizzy, and I threw up. They rushed me to the hospital, and the next day the doctors told me I had a herniated disc. It happened in April, and I had to leave the team. They put me in traction, and I stayed at home with Betty and Kevin. After a week, when I didn't get any better, they decided to operate.

At the time, back surgery was not as advanced as it is today, and in my case it turned into a near disaster. I never found out what went wrong, but I won't forget that day in the hospital. As soon as I was rolled into the operating room a nurse gave me a shot, and I started getting groggy. A few minutes later, someone put a mask over my face and asked me to count backward from one hundred. I don't remember even getting to ninety before I blacked out. I don't know what happened then—either the operation went on longer than they expected, or the anesthetic wasn't strong enough—but I woke up right in the middle of surgery. It was like some scary dream. I was lying on my stomach on the operating table when I opened my eyes and tried to raise up. Then I heard the doctor shouting, "Hurry, get the mask on his face, quick. Hurry! Hold him down, don't let him sit up."

That's the last thing I remember.

Later, as I lay in bed recuperating, I realized how lucky I'd been. I was only twenty-three years old, and I could have been permanently injured or perhaps even could have died on that table. Afterward, all I could do was pray and thank the Lord.

I was laid up for two months. And although I would have preferred playing ball, finishing the season with the team, I enjoyed the time with Betty and my son Kevin. We were living in a cozy one-bedroom apartment in Cincinnati then, and it was one of the best periods of our marriage. Betty was a devoted mother and wife. I know it was tough for her since Kevin was only two years old and I was as much a burden as he was. For me, it wasn't just physical. I was really depressed about my injury, concerned that I might never play basketball again. Betty's encouragement helped keep me going. I don't know how she did it, but somehow she managed to take care of both Kevin and me until I got back on my feet.

That summer, we went back to Baton Rouge to live with Betty's parents, and I started rehab at the Southern University facilities. At first I was just stretching and swimming. Then I began running, and by August I was back on the court doing some light workouts. I took it slow because I was afraid of reinjuring my back, but I came around more quickly than even I expected. At the end of August, I felt pretty confident that I would be able to play the next season.

Almost a Buccaneer

That was the summer of 1967, and earlier in the year owners and promoters of the new American Basketball Association (ABA) had announced that the league would begin play that year. Before the Royals started their training camp, representatives from the New Orleans Buccaneers approached me. Rick Barry had already agreed to leave the NBA's San Francisco franchise and play for the ABA's Oakland team. And the New York playground legend Connie Hawkins, who'd been banned from the NBA, had signed with the Pittsburgh Pipers, the team that eventually won the first ABA title. The league looked like it might be stable and competitive, and I figured I might have a better chance there. So when the Buccaneers offered me a contract for $16,000 in August, twice the amount the Royals were paying me, I agreed to play for them.

When Cincinnati's management discovered that I'd signed with an ABA team, they were furious. The NBA was determined not to lose any more players to the new league. They filed a suit against the Buccaneers for tampering, and my contract was voided. I was told that I had to play in Cincinnati. Then, after I reported to camp, the Royals offered to renegotiate my contract. I signed a one-year deal for a little less than $16,000.

Back to Cincinnati

I was still hurting during training camp and for much of the early part of the season, so I didn't get very much playing time at the start. But my minutes increased after Hairston was traded to Detroit. Considering the injury, it wasn't a bad year. The team's record was about the same as the previous year, but because Seattle and San Diego had come into the league, increasing the number of teams to twelve, we didn't make the play-offs. Again I finished the season averaging around 6 points a game.

I wasn't thrilled with my performance, but when we went home in the spring of 1968, I felt that I was on the verge of becoming the same player that I was in college. That spring, I left Cincinnati, feeling that next year I would make a real contribution to the team. I was looking forward to returning and playing with Oscar.

8

JUNIOR JOURNEYMAN

I knew I was ready to blossom as a player,
but all of a sudden it seemed that I was the
only one who believed in my ability.

THE NBA WAS CHANGING RAPIDLY in 1967. The league was being challenged by the ABA, and the competition was driving player salaries higher and higher. Although the ABA lost out on college superstars like Wes Unseld and Elvin Hayes that year, the bidding for high draft picks was heated and NBA teams were under a lot of pressure. The NBA was also expanding. It had increased from nine to ten teams during the 1966–67 season when Chicago came back into the league. Two more teams were added the following year, and, with new franchises in Milwaukee and Phoenix, there would be fourteen teams at the start of the 1968–69 season.

When Milwaukee and Phoenix were admitted to the league, NBA officials announced that there would be an expansion draft to help provide those teams with quality players. Each of the twelve teams had to select two players from their rosters and make them available for the draft. The new teams could choose any of the twenty-four players in the pool. At first, I wasn't worried about being put up for the expansion draft. Everybody seemed pleased with my improvement, and I'd done well in the limited minutes I'd played the year before. During that summer, Oscar and I practiced together, and he also felt I was one of the players the Royals wanted to keep. But a month or two before training camp was supposed to begin, I heard rumors that I was one of the guys Cincinnati had put up for the draft pool.

Oscar and I had really become tight by then, and he told me that he actually went to the Royals general manager and asked him to protect me in the draft. I know that he felt that I was ready to bust out as a top-notch NBA player, and he thought I would help the team during the coming season. But despite his protests, the Royals didn't protect me, and before the season began I was picked as one of the Milwaukee Bucks draft choices.

Layover in Milwaukee

The truth is, I was heartbroken. I felt that playing with Oscar, I would have reached my potential during that year. But since I had no choice, I reported to the Milwaukee Bucks in the fall, and I led the team in scoring during the exhibition season. I averaged about 19 points a game, and I was confident that the Bucks were pleased with my performance. Although I missed my former teammates in Cincinnati, I had begun to like Milwaukee—it was a clean, quiet little town. The Bucks management was determined to build a competitive team, and coach Larry Costello seemed to like the way I played.

Then, a few weeks after the regular season began, I got a call from John Erickson, the Bucks general manager. He said he wanted me to talk with Wayne Embry, the starting center. Wayne told me that they had asked him to tell me I was being cut. At first, I couldn't believe it.

"H-how ca-can they cu-cu-cut me?" I asked. "I le-led the team in sc-sco-scoring. I sh-sh-should be st-sta-starting."

Wayne said he didn't understand it either, but he had heard that New York wanted to move Cazzie Russell and Milwaukee was trying to get him to fill the forward spot. I was crushed. It didn't make sense to me, because when I had faced Cazzie during the previous season, I ate him alive. When I left that room after talking with Wayne, it seemed that everything I'd worked for had vanished. I knew I was ready to blossom as a player, but all of a sudden it seemed that I was the only one who believed in my ability.

The next day, John Erickson came to my apartment. He didn't beat around the bush. "Bob, we're going to have to cut you, son," he said. "We've got a chance to get Cazzie Russell from the Knicks. I know that you led the team in scoring during preseason play, and I'm sorry that we have to let you go, Bob. But we think Cazzie is a better fit for the team."

He made it clear that Milwaukee was dead set on getting Cazzie, so my performance during the exhibition season didn't matter. As it turned out, they never did get him. He played in New York for two more years before being traded to San Francisco.

I tried to convince Erickson that I could help the team, but he wouldn't listen to any of my arguments. I know that I was excited and stumbling over my words, and I guess that during the discussion things heated up a little. Finally, Erickson lost his patience. And although I don't remember his exact words, I'll never forget what he told me that day. The gist was that I was a pretty good ballplayer, but because I stuttered, I'd never be able to fit in with the Bucks. I was stunned, and I must have sat there trying to stammer out a reply for over a minute. "See, that's the problem, Bob. How do you expect to help us when you can't communicate?"

I was angry and frustrated, but somehow I managed to get a few words out then. I practically begged him to at least try to trade me. He looked at me for a minute or so and finally said, "Ok, I'll try. There is a team that just might take you. They have a player we need anyway. Maybe we can work out a deal for Flynn Robinson with Chicago."

Next Stop: Chicago

I started the season with Milwaukee, but shortly afterward the trade was arranged. They sent me and Bobby Weiss to Chicago for Robinson, who had been a teammate of mine in Cincinnati before he was traded the previous year. I wasn't happy about moving again, but that's part of being a pro athlete—you never know where you'll be playing from one year to the next. At least, I thought, I was going to a team that wanted me. But after Bobby and I reported to the Bulls, I found out that I was wrong about that, too.

It turned out that Chicago wasn't really interested in me at all. I was just a last minute "throw-in" to sweeten the deal. They really wanted Weiss, a left-handed guard out of Penn State who was in his fourth year in the league. He wasn't a great player, but the word around the league was that he was an "intelligent" ballplayer, a steady kind of guy who could handle the ball, run the plays, and wouldn't hurt you coming off the bench. I'd found a new team, but my future didn't look any better there than it had in Milwaukee.

Then about ten days after I arrived in Chicago, I was involved in an auto accident. My second son, Kelly, had just been born, and Betty and I were driving back home with him at about eleven o'clock at night. Suddenly, at the corner of 51st and State, a car ran the light and slammed into us out of nowhere. I didn't see it until the last second, and at the moment of impact I threw myself across the seat to protect Betty and the baby. I was thrown up against the windshield, banging my head and cracking the glass. The last thing I remember seeing was Betty and the baby being hurled against the passenger side window.

It was scary, and all of us wound up with a lot of scratches and bruises. Kelly also broke his leg, Betty broke her nose, and besides aggravating my neck and back, I had a gash on my head and a mild concussion. We were all lucky to have survived without serious injury. But a few weeks later, I discovered that at least in terms of basketball, the accident had been a blessing in disguise.

Although the season had just begun, it seems that Chicago was planning to cut me. After the accident, I was placed on the injured reserve list and they were unable to drop me. Then by the time I was able to play, a few key starters had been injured, and they changed their minds. I stuck with the team, and began to get some playing time by the end of the season. The Bulls missed the play-offs that year, finishing the season with a record of 33–49. Again, I was used primarily for defense and finished the year averaging about 6 points a game. Bob Boozer, the center, was the team's high scorer with over 21 per game.

I was determined to get back in top shape before the start of the next season, so I practiced throughout the summer. I played in the summer league at Chicago's Dr. Martin Luther King Jr. Boys Club. The league was a lot like the Rucker tournament in New York. All the top college players came in there to test their games against the pros. That's where I really got my game together. I got my confidence back and led the league in scoring that summer. By the time training camp opened, I had started playing the way I'd played in college. I knew I could make a strong contribution to the Bulls.

A New Start with the Bulls

At camp, I found out that the team had made a lot of changes during the off-season. They traded Jimmy Washington and Bob Boozer, and brought in Bob Kauffman, a 6-foot 9-inch forward from Seattle. They also picked up Chet Walker, another forward, that year. They seemed determined to build a strong team, but with the addition of two new forwards my place in the rotation was in jeopardy. Walker had been a 20-plus scorer in Philadelphia for several years, and Kauffman was known for punishing people under the basket. Bob was muscular, weighed about 260 pounds, and was strong as an ox. He was a rugged rebounder—a little like Karl Malone, but without Malone's moves or shot. They thought he was going to be a star, but he really couldn't score consistently.

I played very well during training camp and the exhibition season, but at the start of the season I was still coming off the bench subbing either at forward or for our center, Tom Boerwinkle. Kauffman was starting, and we began the year playing poorly and losing. Still, every time coach Dick Motta put me in the game, I'd end up with double figures. The team seemed to have more energy with me in the lineup, and when Kauffman got hurt, Motta was almost forced to give me a shot as a starter.

97

And once he started me, I never looked back. Chet Walker and I tied as team scoring leaders during the 1969–70 season with 21 points per game. And during the seven full years I spent in Chicago, I averaged over 23 points a game, leading the Bulls in scoring for a record seven straight years. That record stood until the 1990s, when it was broken by the greatest player of all time, Michael Jordan.

Although Dick Motta and I had an off-and-on relationship over the years, I always gave him credit for giving me the opportunity to become a starter. Motta was as stubborn and hottempered as I was on the basketball court, so there were personality clashes along the way. Sometimes we were at each other's throats. But he was determined to build a winning team in Chicago—so despite our differences, as long as he felt I could contribute to that goal we managed to get along.

Motivation, Motta Style

Dick Motta was tough, abrasive, didn't mince words—and on the court, he didn't give a damn about anybody's feelings. Sometimes that approach motivated the team. I remember a game that we played against New York around the Christmas holidays. It was during the early '70s, when the Knicks had those great teams with Walt Frazier, Earl "the Pearl" Monroe, Jerry Lucas, Bill Bradley, Dick Barnett, Phil Jackson, Willis Reed, and Dave DeBusschere. They were red-hot when they came out— couldn't miss. They made every shot they threw, and at halftime they had us down by more than 20 points.

For them it was a laugher, one of those games where it seemed as if they were moving at high speed and we were in slow motion. I made a few shots, but before the break I was really pitiful. When we went back to the locker rooms, Motta was steaming. He called us spineless and gutless, said we didn't have any heart. Then he started singling out individual players. When he got to me, he said, "Love, you let DeBusschere keep you off the boards. You let Lucas score at will. Jackson pushed you all over the court. Where's your pride? They manhandled you, pushed you right out of your game." Then he looked at me, waved his hands in disgust, and said, "You just can't play against a good team! None of you can."

What did he say that for? My blood started boiling. I was fuming. I couldn't wait to get back out on the floor. Motta must have seen how I reacted, seen something in my eyes, because as we huddled up just before the horn blew for the third quarter, he turned to Norm Van Lier. "I want you to get the ball to Butter," he said, "every time down the court. Let's see what he can do."

And sure enough, on our first eight or nine possessions they got the ball to me. Each time, I turned and either drove to the hoop or went up for the jumper. I hit six or seven of those shots, and that set the tone for the rest of the game. We cut the lead down to about 12 points at the end of third quarter. New York went cold. We were pressing them defensively, and they started turning the ball over. They couldn't hit a thing, and we were getting rebounds and pushing the ball down on the break. They couldn't stop us.

During my career, I prided myself on being in better shape than most of the guys I played against. Most nights, at the beginning of the fourth quarter, I felt as though I was just beginning to play. And on that night, I was sizzling in the last period. I was posting guys up, driving to the hoop, and draining shots from fifteen, twenty feet. We climbed back into that game and won by one point. It was a complete team effort; everybody stepped up their games and contributed in the second half. It was one of the greatest games I ever played in, and that was partly because the coach challenged us.

99

OddBulls

Under Motta, Chicago was a hard-nosed, tough defensive team—a physical, blue-collar outfit. We tried to punish the opposing teams, and nobody was afraid to get a little blood on his uniform. Jerry Sloan, Norm Van Lier, Chet Walker, Tom Boerwinkle, and I were the nucleus of the team during most of the eight years I played in Chicago. But there were other players like Clifford Ray, Howard Porter, Bobby Weiss, Bobby Wilson, Garfield Heard, Matt Goukas, and Nate Thurmond who came through and helped establish the team's style and character.

Basically, we were a rough and tough, scrappy team that always fought hard, especially on defense. And although we ran whenever we got the chance, we usually stuck to a controlled halfcourt offense. Jerry Sloan and Norm Van Lier were two of the most intense guys I ever played with, and that intensity sometimes led to a lot of scraps and ejections on the court and even some blowups in the locker room. They were outspoken players, explosive, and they could sometimes be a little hot-headed. And if I hadn't had my speech problem, I would probably have been just as loud. I didn't say much, but I think they knew that when push came to shove, I was right there with them.

As it happened, my contractual disputes with coach Motta and the Bulls management added to the fire on the court. After a while, it seemed that we were getting almost as much attention for our off-court behavior as we were for our play. Sportswriters started calling the team "volatile," "unpredictable," and "eccentric." Bill Gleason, a reporter from the *Chicago Sun-Times*, even took to calling us the "OddBulls." And with some of the rowdy, raucous crowds that came into the old Chicago Stadium, most teams that stepped onto our home court knew they faced a rough night.

"They call us dirty, everywhere we go," Norm Van Lier told a reporter. "Chicago is the only place in the league where our style of play is understood and appreciated. Everywhere else they think we're animals." There was a lot of truth in what he said. Most of the time, there was a circuslike atmosphere at the arena. It was raucous, and opposing teams always knew that each of us would fight to the last minute and leave everything we had on the court.

Guys You Just Didn't Want to Mess With

It wasn't just Chicago—the whole league was rougher back in that era. Players lift all kinds of weights today, and they look strong and intimidating. But none of them really wants to fight. When we played, there were fists flying, knuckles to the head. Nowadays, all these guys do is shove or push. They'll get up in your face and woof, but then they back up and start yelling, "Don't hold me back, don't hold me back!" Most of the time, it's just a big show. In the '60s and '70s, nobody backed down. If you did, everybody would run over you.

On our team, Jerry Sloan was one of the toughest players out there, and he was known for taking charges. Opposing players hated it. One time when we were playing the Knicks at Chicago Stadium, it led to some trouble. Willis Reed was hurt, but he was playing anyway. And every time down the court, Jerry would step in front of him, trying to draw a charge. Reed was getting tired of it; you could see it on his face. Then in the second quarter, after he got a rebound and threw the outlet pass, Reed was running up the court and didn't see Jerry step in front of him. Jerry took the charge, and both of them went down hard. Reed was hurt badly, almost had tears in his eyes, and he was called for the foul. When Jerry went to the foul line, Reed shouted, "Motherfucker, don't you ever step in front of me again. You hurt my knee."

A few plays later, Reed was hobbling down the court to the defensive end when Jerry stepped in front of him again. Reed acted like he didn't see him, then at the last minute sped up, put his shoulder down, and hit Jerry like a Mack truck. Flattened him. We had to take Jerry out of the game. "I warned you," Reed said, as they helped Jerry off the court, "don't ever step in front of me again."

Even though Jerry was limping, he looked back and said, "You didn't hurt me." Reed just smiled.

There were a lot of guys you just didn't want to mess with, not if you had good sense. Wilt Chamberlain and Bill Russell, for instance, were guys you didn't want to embarrass or irritate on the court. They had a lot of pride, and they could be mean as hell. If you made them look bad, they made you pay for it.

I remember a game back in my rookie year when we played doubleheaders during the exhibition season. We played first, and afterward we hung around to watch the second game.

Wilt and Philadelphia were facing the St. Louis Hawks. The Hawks had Zelmo Beaty, a 6-foot 9-inch center who weighed about 240 or 250 pounds. He was a good, hard-nosed player, and from as far back as his college days with Prairie View, he had a reputation as a tough defender who would hurt you in the post. Wilt, of course, was over 7 feet tall and weighed about 300 pounds. And because he was never a good free-throw shooter, teams always fouled him. It was the only way to stop him for most teams.

So from the opening tipoff, every time Wilt got the ball, Zelmo fouled him. He was hammering Wilt, and Wilt was missing nearly every foul shot. The crowd was laughing and booing, and you could see Wilt getting madder and madder. Then about ten minutes into the game, Wilt went up for a dunk, and Zelmo got him with a particularly hard foul—caught him around the neck with his forearm as he reached in to block the shot. Wilt glared at Zelmo, and on the way down the court after he missed one of two free throws, he caught up with him and said, "Zelmo, I'm warning you, don't hit me like that again." You could see Wilt pointing his finger as he trotted down the court.

The very next time down the court, Zelmo fouled him again. Wilt missed the dunk and had to go up to the free-throw line. Both shots rolled off the rim. The crowd was roaring with laughter and Wilt was steaming. When he got back to the offensive end, he started yelling, "Gimme the ball. Gimme the damn ball!" He got the pass, faked, and, took a long stride toward the basket, right into Zelmo's chest. Zelmo went up but he couldn't reach the ball; he came down with both hands and hit Wilt square in the face. That's when Wilt blew up. He charged, and Zelmo took off toward the stands. He was about five rows up the stairs when Wilt caught up and grabbed him by his ankle.

Zelmo was kicking and struggling to get loose, and Wilt was pounding him on his back, his legs, anywhere he could reach. Zelmo started kicking and rolling around in the aisle, trying to get away, but Wilt was a strong man. He wouldn't turn him loose. It took all the players from both teams to pull Wilt off him, and I don't remember anybody fouling him the rest of the night.

There were some furious clashes back in those days, and the old Bulls fit right into that roughhouse atmosphere. For several years, we challenged the league's best teams.

9

A RUN WITH THE BULLS

*That stretch from 1970 to 1975 was the best
period of my pro career.*

BEGINNING WITH THE 1970–71 SEASON, we had a run of five
years during which we were serious contenders for the title.
Despite the dissension that made headlines in the press, we
won over fifty games in an eight-two game schedule four years
in a row. Each of those years, we finished second behind Milwaukee in the Midwest Division of the NBA's Western Conference. Oscar had been traded to the Bucks in 1970, and with
Kareem Abdul-Jabbar at center they had one of the league's
best teams. They went to the finals twice during the four years
Oscar played in Milwaukee, and in 1971 they beat Baltimore
and won the title. We finally won the division title in 1975, the
year after Oscar retired. That was the year that we had our best
run at a championship. But the Golden State Warriors defeated
us in a tight, hard-fought seven-game series in the semifinals.
Golden State went on to beat Washington and win the 1974–75
title.

"The Bulls Most Tenacious Defender"

That stretch from 1970 to 1975 was the best period of my pro
career. We had a terrific team, but we never could quite get
over the hump and get to the finals, although we got close a few
times. Thinking back about those years, I always remember the
individual matchups. There were some great players in the NBA

at that time, and since I was always trying to prove myself, fighting for respect on the court and with the Bulls front office, I was at my best when I faced them. I was a scorer, and I could shoot—but I prided myself on defense. And since I always watched the best forward on the other team, I was guarding a superstar almost every night.

Two of the best were Elgin Baylor and Rick Barry. They were also among the most difficult to guard. Baylor was 6 feet 5 inches and weighed about 220 pounds—strong as a bull. Although he wasn't that tall, he was one of the league's top rebounders. But he was also quick and handled the ball like a guard. He was the Michael Jordan of his era. In the '60s and '70s, he was driving and hanging in the air just like Michael did in the '90s. I faced him after he had knee surgery, and he couldn't elevate or dunk like Michael then, but he was probably a better shooter. And as if that weren't enough, Baylor had this deceptive nervous tic.

Every time he ran down the court, he would jerk his neck to one side or the other. You never knew if it was a fake or just the nervous condition. He would just stand there and guys would be leaning back on their heels. When I came into the league, I really didn't know about the tic, and every time he bobbed his head or jerked his neck, I would slide backward or jump. Even after I realized what was going on, it was almost impossible to stop him. He made you work harder than any player I faced. I had blisters for two or three days after every game with Los Angeles when he was playing. All during those games I was stopping, sliding, and jumping. Baylor was one of the greatest players of all time, and when he retired in 1971, everyone who had ever guarded him was relieved.

Rick Barry was a totally different kind of player. He was an excellent long-range shooter and an excellent passer. If the NBA had the three-point shot during the '70s, Barry would probably have averaged 10 more points a game. He was one of those players who moved constantly without the ball, and they set all kinds of picks for him. The Warriors had guys like Bill Bridges and Clifford Ray on their team in the mid-'70s, and after you ran into those guys all night long you always went home bruised and hurting. Still, we had some great duels when we faced each other, and although we were usually neck and neck, Barry was one of the few guys who outscored me when we were matched up.

There were other guys who gave me fits when I guarded them. A lot of them were guards or centers I was occasionally matched against. They included some of the greatest players of all time: Jerry West, Pete Maravich, Willis Reed, Walt Frazier, Bob McAdoo, Earl Monroe, Wilt Chamberlain, and, after I left Cincinnati, even Oscar. Of course, nobody could stop those guys. But in matchups against the league's premier forwards, I usually came out on top. I loved to play against Spencer Haywood, John Havlicek, Elvin Hayes, Connie Hawkins, Gus Johnson, and Billy Cunningham. And most times, on an individual basis, l came out on top.

One reason for my success was that when I first came into the league, they really didn't know me. I was usually put in the lineup for defense, so they didn't have any respect for my offensive game. I got a lot of easy hoops. Then, after the 1970–71 season, when I was selected to the All-Pro team for the first time, I always tried to motivate myself with the thought that I wasn't getting the publicity and respect I deserved from the writers. So every time I faced the top players, I tried to psyche myself into having a great game—on offense and defense. I felt I had something to prove when I went up against those guys. It kept me on edge, kept that fire burning. And I always believed that if you wanted to be successful in anything you had to have that competitive edge.

Nothing made me prouder than when sportswriters began calling me "the Bulls' most tenacious defender." And I felt that whenever the player I guarded had to guard me, I always had the advantage. There were exceptions like Gus Johnson, Jerry West, and John Havlicek, but many of the league's high-scoring stars either couldn't or didn't like to play defense. And if they were forced to guard another good offensive player, their point total went down. I'd learned early on that moving without the ball was the key to good offense, and most players who guarded me would tire as the game went on. Every time down the court, I ran a series of figure-eight routes through three or four picks. I never stopped, and usually I wore them down. As one Chicago writer pointed out, that constant motion became a part of my defense in one-on-one duels.

My Offensive Game

I loved playing defense, but don't get me wrong—I also thought of myself as a scorer. In Chicago, I had some differences with Dick Motta, and I always felt that deep down in his heart he didn't like me or respect my game. Still, once he put me in the lineup, he made me the first or second option on offense. It was a forward-oriented offense, so usually Chet Walker or I got the call. Motta wanted me to shoot, and he didn't care how often I did it. That suited me just fine, because I loved to take the ball to the hoop.

Although I didn't shoot quite as much as guys like Rick Barry, I was right up there with the leaders in field goal attempts. For a time around the early '70s, there was even a joke about me going around the NBA: guys used to say, "Love could be in a phone booth with Wilt Chamberlain and still think he was open."

Still, I was never strictly a one-on-one ballplayer. I was a good post-up player, so when I was guarded by a small forward, I could take my man inside and use my height, shoot little hook shots. And with the bigger guys, I tried to take them outside and slip picks for the quick jumper that Oscar had helped me develop. They were usually slower, so if they pressed me out there I made a little move—feint left, then right—to get off the jumper or go around them.

The guys who made it toughest for me to score were Gus "Honeycomb" Johnson, who played with the Baltimore Bullets, and Bill Bridges, who played with the Hawks in St. Louis and

Atlanta. Gus was a good offensive player and a great rebounder. He could leap as high as anybody. But he was also strong as a bull. And when he guarded you, he could just muscle you out of position. He was the only guy in the league who could say, "Don't move. I want you to stay right there," then put his index finger on you and keep you there. He was powerful—had the strongest hands, wrists, and arms I've ever seen. On defense, Bridges played a lot like Gus. He had fingers like the limbs on a tree. His hands were so strong that he could move most guys around like they were straw men. Neither of them was really quick, but back in those days you could use your hands to push or check a guy, and they were masters at slowing you down.

Still, I was a difficult player to guard even for those guys because I was moving without the ball all the time, and once I got away from them they couldn't catch up. I always saw the floor really well, saw how a play was developing, and usually I made the right cut. Most of my shots came off screens and pick-and-rolls. They came out of a team offense and usually involved an assist from another player.

I think that's why the Knicks' Bill Bradley was one of the players who really respected my play. We had similar games. He was a great shooter who was always in motion and worked the picks as well as anyone who played. He was a fierce competitor, but he was also a gentleman and one of the most intelligent players to ever step on the court. Back in the '70s he told an interviewer that I was one of the smartest players he had ever played against; I thought that was the ultimate compliment. Bradley was a student of the game. He came into the league a year before I did, and we both retired after the 1976–77 season. Over the years, we faced each other dozens of times, and I came to respect his style of play. I often guarded him, because we needed someone who could stay with him when he ran all those patterns and tried to come off the screens. He always ran me ragged. Most of the time, they put one of the roughhouse guys on me—DeBusschere or Phil Jackson, their defensive specialist. Still, I usually had great games in New York. They tried to rough me up, but it didn't work. And I think Bradley's remarks reflect how much he respected me for the type of game I brought to the court on defense and offense.

"The Most Underrated Player in the League"

During my NBA career, I didn't always get that kind of respect from the press, management, or the players I faced, even though the stats show that I was right up there with the best of them. In 1975, near the end of my career, one writer did speak out. "Love has been the Bulls' top scorer ever since he began to play regularly," Robert Markus wrote in the *Chicago Tribune*. "He is also the team's top defensive forward and one of the best in the league. There are few two-way performers in the NBA in a class with Love. Yet he is probably the least-publicized player on his own team." He went on to quote a player who called me "the most underrated player in the league" and argued that due to my speech impediment, the electronic media had an excuse for overlooking me—but he and the other writers did not.

After I left the league, I began to realize how much my speech problem had influenced others' opinions of me. People just assume that if you can't communicate or speak well, you're stupid. It's like the old cliché, deaf and *dumb*. That stereotype colors the way people look at you. Most of them can't get past it. And even the people who don't think you're stupid feel awkward when they're around you. I guess it's uncomfortable for a lot of them. They feel sorry for you or they're embarrassed. Either way, it's hard for them to respect you, and they tend to back off.

Even during my best years in the league—1971 and 1972, when I averaged over 25 points a game and was selected to the All-Pro teams—sportswriters tended to avoid me. Some nights, after I'd scored 30 or 40 points, the writers would come into the locker room and look right past me. They went straight to another player for a quote or comment on the game. And I always felt that my contract battles with Dick Motta and the Bulls owners, Jonathan Kovler and Arthur Wirtz, stemmed from the lack of respect they had for my contributions to the team. I was not only the lowest-paid NBA All-Star in basketball, but also one of the lowest-paid players among the Bulls starters.

Although I got along with most of the other players, there were a few in the league who either snubbed me or avoided me in social situations. It's only natural, I guess. A lot of people really don't know what to do when they're around a person with a disability. And though I didn't think of myself that way at the time, once I left the glitter of the pro sports arena, I was forced to confront my disability.

It was easy to ignore while I was still playing basketball. And, as I've said, I tried to use other people's negative views to gain an edge on the court. I was driven to excel against the best players. I wanted to prove that I was every bit as good as they were and deserved to be paid and respected as much as they were. I also got up for all the games with the top teams. Against Philadelphia, Golden State, Los Angeles, Boston, and New York, I was usually at my best. And I was never more determined than when we played the Milwaukee Bucks.

I never forgot the conversation I had with the Bucks general manager before I was traded. And after Oscar was traded to them and they won the title in 1971, I kept thinking that I could've been on that team with him and Kareem. We would have been unbeatable. Every time we played Milwaukee, I'd think about what was said when they decided to cut me. We played them a few dozen times while I was with Chicago, and I always used that as a motivating factor. I had great games against them. Every time we played, I tried to put up 30 or 40 points.

I'll never forget the night in 1973 when I scored 49 points against them at Chicago Stadium. Besides Oscar and Kareem, they had Bobby Dandridge, Curtis Perry, and Lucius Allen. It was a strong team, and they went on to win the division title. But that particular night, I went on a tear. From the moment I stepped on the court, the basket looked as big as an ocean. It was as if I was looking down at it all night long; I could actually see inside the hoop.

Nobody could stop me that night. I did it all. I went back door, hit twenty-five–foot jumpers, took Dandridge and Perry into the paint and posted up. At one point in the game I got so hot they put Kareem on me. Still, they couldn't stop me. Even though I wasn't that tall, I had a variety of deceptive moves under the hoop, and I could post up much taller players. A lot of teams had their centers guard me, and except for maybe Wilt or Russell, it didn't matter. I hit on nearly 60 percent of my shots that night, and we beat Milwaukee 123–99.

After the game, when I saw one of the Milwaukee execs in the corridor, I walked up to him and said, "Si-sir, I-I'm st-st-still trying to f-fi-find the guy who c-ca-can talk the ball into the b-ba-basket. Did y-you fi-find one y-y-yet?"

During my seven and a half years with the Bulls, I was voted onto the NBA All-Pro team twice, I was a four-time All-Star team selection, and I averaged over 23 points a game, leading the Bulls in scoring for seven consecutive years and establishing nearly all of their scoring records. We went from cellar dwellers to contenders two years after I arrived, and the team finished with winning records five times during my career. I was proud of my accomplishments in the NBA, but like most pro athletes, I hungered for a championship ring. The Bulls never made it during the '70s, and I'll always regret that we didn't get it the one time when we came closest to grabbing that ring.

A Final Run for the Roses

We won the division title during the 1974–75 season, and after defeating Kansas City in six games, we faced Golden State for the Western Conference title. We were one series away from going to the finals and playing the Eastern Conference champs. I was in top form and had averaged 22 points a game that year. And while Chet Walker was hurting with a pulled muscle, most of our team was physically ready. I could almost taste the championship. I'd never been more confident about our chances.

We got off on the wrong foot when we lost the opening game of the series 107–89 at the Coliseum Arena in Oakland. I had a hot hand, scoring 37 points, but the rest of the team was cold and Rick Barry buried us with 38 points. Then we returned to Chicago and won both games. We were up 2–1 when we went back to the West Coast, and the fourth play-off game turned out to be pivotal. We were sailing along with a lead of 19 points in the third quarter, but the Warriors came storming back and beat us 111–106. Still, when we won the fifth game 89–79 to go up 3–2, we all felt that we could end it in the sixth game at Chicago Stadium. But Golden State won a tight sixth game, 86–72.

The last game was back in Oakland, and everybody on our team knew that we had our backs against the wall. Again we got off to a good start, and led by 14 points at one time. But the Warriors battled back, tied the score, then took the lead in the fourth quarter with a couple of minutes left. It was neck and neck during the last few minutes, but finally Golden State eked out an 83–79 win.

That was one of the most disappointing games I ever played. I finished the series with a 23-point average, but in that last game I had one of my worst offensive days in the NBA. I shot 6 of 26 from the floor and scored only 17 points. It was a game that we should have won, and I left the arena knowing that even if I'd had an average shooting night, the Bulls would have gone on to play for the championship.

It was hard to believe that we lost, and on the plane ride back to Chicago you could almost feel the frustration. We blew it, and all of us were angry and let down. It was months before I could even think about next year. But by the summer, I began trying to gear myself up for the 1975–76 season. I would turn thirty-three years old during the following season, but physically I felt pretty good, and I was looking forward to making another run at the title. I had no idea that the team we had built the previous year would fall apart, or that it would be my last full year with the Bulls.

10

MY FINAL YEAR IN THE NBA

*It seemed that my NBA career was over, and it
all had happened so suddenly that I had no
plans for the future.*

THE 1975–76 SEASON STARTED OFF badly when my contract
dispute with the Bulls reared up during training camp. I
knew that I only had a few more productive years in the
league, and since I was one of the lowest-paid players on the
team, I had asked my lawyer to renegotiate my contract. He had
tried the year before, but I'd finally given in and played under
the old deal. This time I was determined, and it got to be a very
messy situation because a rift had developed between Dick
Motta and a few of the other players, including me.

The bad feelings had started when we lost the seventh game
to Golden State in the 1974–75 conference series. Afterward,
Motta told the team that Norm Van Lier and I didn't deserve
full play-off shares because our holdouts earlier in the year had
cost our team the championship. He argued that if we had
started the season, the Bulls would have won more games, and
therefore would have had home-court advantage against the
Warriors. Our teammates didn't agree, and we got our full
shares. Still, there was some resentment, and a lot of us never
forgot those comments.

During the summer of 1975, Chet Walker said he wouldn't
play another year under Motta and announced that he was
retiring. And during the preseason, both Van Lier and I asked
for raises. They settled with him early, but my dispute continued after the season began. Finally, in November, after I had

been benched for a few games and suspended for a short time, they offered a new contract. By that time, the team had gotten off to a terrible start and the split between Motta and me had widened. It got worse during the rest of the season.

Injuries plagued the team from the start. Both Jerry Sloan and Van Lier got hurt early in the season, and I had an ankle injury and then a back problem that got worse as the season progressed. Van Lier recovered, but, playing hurt for much of the year, his average dropped from 15 points to 12 points a game. Sloan was more seriously injured and only played in twenty-two games. It was his last year as a player in the NBA. Our starting five had been the oldest team in the league when we went to the semifinals the previous year, and it seemed that time was catching up with us. Walker was gone, and except for our center, Tom Boerwinkle, the rest of us were definitely hurting. Still, I always felt that it was a lack of team morale as much as the injuries that killed us that year.

We opened the season with 3 wins and 10 losses, and things did not get much better. With all the clubhouse dissension and my contract dispute, the press had a field day. All those stories about "eccentrics" and "oddbulls" returned to the headlines. It seemed like the whole city was down on us. The team was frustrated, and Motta was at the end of his rope. Whatever else you might say about him, there was never any doubt that the man wanted to win. So behind the locker room doors, things went from bad to worse.

We tried to regroup, but there was just not enough fight in our team to overcome the injuries. The chemistry wasn't there. Near the end of the season, I was getting cortisone shots before every game for what the trainer said was tendinitis in my knees. It was painful, but I tried to play through it. And since we were losing regularly, I began trying to take on more of the scoring load than I should have. I don't know whether it was the injury or just forcing bad shots, but my field goal percentage dropped to an all-time low. Motta cut down on my minutes and even benched me for a few games in March, which increased the tension between us. By the end of the season, we had suffered a nearly complete collapse. We finished the year with 24 wins and 58 losses, the worst record of any Chicago team I'd played for and the worst in the league that year.

I averaged 19 points a game and led the team in scoring, but I knew that if Motta stayed in Chicago I would be traded or cut before the next season. He was director of player personnel as well as the coach, and too much had gone down between us. I always felt that he blamed me and the contract dispute for much of the dissension on the team. And while I thought he had come to respect my game, I knew he hated my independence. Like a lot of coaches in that era, he treated players almost like children. He expected them to accept everything he said without question. But things were changing in professional sports. Players were beginning to speak out and object to being treated like cattle. They called us rebellious and volatile back then, but I think that Bulls team was just an example of the change that was coming.

Reuniting with My Father

The 1975–76 season was a disaster for me and for the Bulls. The only bright spot was that after thirty-three years, I met my father again. I had been trying to find out where he was for years and years, and finally I got word that he was living in Detroit. So when we went to play the Pistons I checked the phone book, and I found his name listed—Benjamin E. Love. I almost fell off my chair when I saw it: Reverend Benjamin E. Love.

I called immediately, and Jevon, one of my younger brothers, answered the phone. I told him who I was and asked could I speak to my father. When he came to the phone and heard me, he started yelling, "Robert Earl, Robert Earl! Is that you?" He was surprised and seemed as happy as I was to hear his voice. It seems that he had followed my career, even gone to a game or two to watch me play, but he was too embarrassed to contact me. There was a lot of guilt on his part, and I guess my call

117

relieved some of it. We really didn't know each other—didn't know what to say. But we talked for about a half hour. He told me that the reason he didn't get in touch with me was that he was ashamed because of all the time that had passed. It was an emotional call, and I was excited about finding him. It's hard to remember exactly what we talked about that evening. But I do know that I invited the whole family out to the game that night.

After the game I took them all out to eat, and we caught up on old times. After all the years that had passed, I really didn't have any hard feelings against him. I respected him as my father. I tried to find out why he left and what he had gone through, and I began to understand why he didn't contact me after all those years. I told him that I was a little shy about calling him, too.

When you're separated from someone—when you don't see or speak to that person for weeks, months, or even years—it becomes more and more difficult to break the ice and face him or her. After a while, you just don't know what to say. I knew that, and I told him that I never really held it against him. I always felt loved as a child. I had my mother and grandmother. I had family and relatives, my uncles and aunts. And I always had a male figure there to help me through hard times. Still, I had missed him, and at the end of that evening I told him that I loved him.

We kept in touch, and during the next few years we became kind of close. I contacted him again once he moved and became pastor of a church in Los Angeles. I even went to hear him preach a bunch of times. But usually we went out to eat, or I went to his house and we sat around and talked. Sometimes I'd even stay a few days, and we hung out together. I was trying to make up for lost time because it just seemed that after so many years, I didn't know him and there was so much to find out. But as much as I tried, there was still something missing. I never really got to know him the way a son should know his father.

In 1988, my father died while I was working up in Seattle. He had been sick for a few months, and I was working and traveling all over the country. I'd promised myself for weeks that I'd get down to Los Angeles. But things got busy, and I kept postponing the trip. I never got a chance to see him before he passed, and I cried like a baby when I heard the news. His funeral was one of the saddest days of my life. It was partly guilt and partly the realization that I would never get to really know him. I just hoped that he knew how much I loved him and respected him as my father. And I was glad that I'd made that phone call back in 1976.

Traded to the Nets

Even though I'd signed a new contract and finally felt that the Bulls were paying me the salary I deserved, I worried about being traded or cut when the 1976 season ended. Then Dick Motta announced that he was leaving, and I felt like someone had given me a reprieve. Motta took a job with the Washington Bullets, and the Bulls started looking for a new coach. A half dozen guys were considered, and one of them was Ed Badger, the coach at Wright College, a junior college in Chicago. There was some resistance to hiring Badger, but I was one of the people who supported him. Whenever the question came up with team officials or the press, I said I thought he'd be a great coach. And that summer, the Bulls hired him.

Chicago made some great moves during the off-season. The ABA had been disbanded after the 1975–76 season, and four of their teams had joined the NBA. Many of the best players from the other teams had also come into the league. One of them, Artis Gilmore, an All-Star center from Kentucky in the ABA, was picked up by the Bulls. They also drafted Scott May, who was the college player of the year at Indiana University. With a new coach and some good young players coming aboard, I was really excited when I went to training camp that year. Physically I was still hurting, but I'd worked out during the summer and I felt as though I still had a few more productive years with the team.

During the exhibition season, my body really began acting up. They kept telling me that I had a knee problem, but I was

119

convinced that it was my back. Later, almost too late, I discovered that I was right. It was painful, and I couldn't go full tilt.
But I kept getting cortisone shots and playing through the pain.
I was sure that I'd get over it. Sloan and Walker were gone, but
with Van Lier, Boerwinkle, the new guys, and me, it looked as
though we had the nucleus for a contending team. Then, about
eight or nine games into the season, I turned on the radio and
heard that I was going to be traded. I couldn't believe it. There
was no warning, and Badger didn't have the decency to tell me
himself. I was hurt and angry. I'd supported him and thought
he was a friend. But he didn't even call me, and later, when I
tried to talk to him, he still didn't explain why they traded me.

Of course, I'll never know, but I suspected that the Bulls had
planned on getting rid of me all along. That suspicion increased
later when I discovered that Badger and Motta had been friends.
And when I talked to my lawyer, I also realized that the contract I'd signed with the team was not a no-cut deal. There was
no salary guarantee. I was furious, but there was nothing that
I could do.

I had been traded to the Nets, one of the ABA teams that had
been absorbed by the NBA, and in November I reported to New
York. Kevin Loughery was the Nets coach, and Bill Melchionni
was the general manager. They were both former players, and
we had faced each other a few times over the years.

Loughery had played for the Bullets when they were in Baltimore until the end of the 1971–72 season. He had been a
fiery, in-your-face kind of guy as a player, and we'd had some
words. He approached his coaching job in much the same way.
In the ABA, he had won a couple of titles after Dr. J joined the
team in 1973, but he was not one of the league's most popular
coaches. Melchionni played for the Philadelphia 76ers when I
first came into the league, but had moved to the ABA and finished his career with the Nets. We were fairly good friends,
and he thought I could contribute to the team.

When I joined the Nets, my back was bothering me and I
wasn't getting much playing time, but I was sure that I could
gradually work myself back into shape. Then, about a month

after I arrived, Kevin Loughery called me into his office and told me I was being dropped. I was hurting. My back was killing me, my leg was killing me. I couldn't really jump. I couldn't do much of anything. But after all those years in the NBA, I thought they would at least put me on the injured reserve list and give me a chance to recuperate. Instead, they cut me.

I was devastated when I returned home. Betty and I were still living in Palatine, Illinois, a suburb about 35 miles north of Chicago, and at that time we had six children. We sat down and talked about my situation, but I was at a loss. It seemed that my NBA career was over, and it all had happened so suddenly that I had no plans for the future. I really didn't know what to do, where to turn.

Then a week or so after I left the Nets, I got a call from my old friend Bill Russell, who was coach of the Seattle Supersonics. He said, "Bob, you don't deserve to go out like this," and asked if I was interested in playing for the Sonics. Of course, I jumped at the chance. I went out there the next day and signed with Seattle. Shortly afterward, Betty and I sold our house in Illinois and moved the family to the West Coast.

Dr. J and the ABA

It was about midseason when I arrived in Seattle, and already it was obvious that the addition of four former ABA teams and many of the stars from the disbanded league was having an effect on the NBA. When the merger was first announced, there was a lot of excitement and anticipation. People wanted to see how teams like San Antonio and Denver and players like George Gervin, Artis Gilmore, Dan Issel, and Julius Erving would do in the NBA. The ABA had always played a looser, more freewheeling style of basketball than the NBA, and by midseason that style was beginning to influence the way games were played and officiated.

I loved the way those guys played on the offensive end. It was inventive, colorful basketball that relied on a fast-paced running game. That style was the forerunner of the 1990s game with Magic Johnson's no-look passes, Michael Jordan's dunks and acrobatic drives, and Allen Iverson's razor-sharp cuts and crossover moves. Although old-guard basketball purists hated it, in my prime I would have been right at home with that style, particularly if they had paid a little more attention to the defensive side. But, at age thirty-four and hurting, I mostly watched when the new guys came into the league.

Julius Erving, Dr. J, was probably the most highly touted former ABA star. Everybody expected him to put some life back into the NBA and bring the fans back with his soaring dunks and flamboyant style of play. And although I only faced him a few times and saw limited time that year, I always looked forward to the matchups with him. He had the reputation of being a really good player. He had those big hands like Connie Hawkins and Michael Jordan, and he was known for soaring to the basket, hanging in the air, and creating shots on the run. Still, I always prided myself on playing tight defense. The first time I faced him was in a game in Philadelphia, and I was determined not to let him dunk on me. Throughout the game, he was scoring with these acrobatic shots—driving, hanging, taking the ball behind his head with one hand, and finishing with scoop shots or kisses off the board. But late in the fourth quarter, he still hadn't dunked on me. So the crowd started chanting, "Doc, Doc, slam dunk! Slam on him, Doc! Slam on him!"

That just made me more determined to keep him from dunking. Philadelphia was winning, and the game had already been decided. But they isolated Dr. J on the side while I was guarding him. He faked, dribbled between his legs, then behind his back, then did a little spin move. I was still with him. Then he feinted to the right and, with a quick move to his left, slipped past me. I knew he was going up for a dunk, and when he left the floor I grabbed him by the forearm and pulled him down. I said, "No way, Doc. You can have the layups. But ain't no way you gonna do no dunking on me tonight." He just laughed.

I never backed down when guarding another player, no matter what kind of reputation he had. And when I faced Doc that year, he never dunked on me. I knew he could leap and had even slammed on Jabbar and other centers, but I just refused to let it happen to me. I was always proud of my defense, and I felt particularly good about that.

The league was changing, and guys like Doc, who took up where Elgin Baylor, Earl Monroe, and Pete Maravich left off, were getting a lot of attention. They probably didn't focus on defense as much as they should have, but they brought a fresh, more spectacular approach to the game, and league officials, fans, and the press were ready for it. There had been guys like me who had many of the same moves. But until the NBA and ABA merged, everybody had kept them on the shelf. Most coaches—guys who had played ten or fifteen years before— wouldn't stand for it. For them, it was too much like the Harlem Globetrotters razzle-dazzle style of play. Plus, a lot of the players looked at it as showboating, and back then, if you showed somebody up you knew you would pay for it the next time down the court. Somebody would knock you on your butt.

But starting with the 1976–77 season, the game began opening up, and Doc was one of the key players who brought in the change. Along with George McGinnis, another ABA player who had switched to the NBA the year before, he led the 76ers to the finals that year. The purists breathed a sigh of relief when Philadelphia lost to Portland in six games, but Doc and his team had shown that showtime basketball could be exciting and competitive. It would become a permanent part of the NBA.

Doc was always a gentleman, on and off the court, and I respected him. I also think that both of us got a lot of respect on the court. But at the end of the 1976–77 season, when I played with Seattle and saw the kind of fanfare the new guys were getting, I couldn't help thinking about the problems I'd had getting respect from the media. Even though most players acknowledged it, my name was rarely brought up when they wrote about the guys who played hardest or toughest at both ends of the court. The speech problem was definitely part of it, since I was seldom interviewed. But I always felt most of the writers never really understood or took notice of my game.

Closing the NBA Chapter of My Life

Seattle had a mediocre record that season. We finished in fourth place in the Pacific Division of the Western Conference with just under a .500 winning percentage. I struggled with my back the entire time out there and averaged a little over 7 points a game. When the season ended, I was convinced that my back injury was more serious than I thought. During the off-season, I tried practicing and exercising to get back in shape, but the pain was just too intense. My back ached and my legs were numb. I couldn't jump, and running was painful. Nothing I did seemed to help. I didn't want to admit it, but it looked as though it was time to give it up. Although I knew I'd miss the thrill and challenge of playing pro ball, the applause of the fans, and the excitement I'd felt every time I left the locker room to go out for the opening tipoff, that fall I decided to retire from the NBA.

When I left the Supersonics, I wasn't sure what I would do next. I still had some deferred payments coming in from the Chicago Bulls, so I wasn't immediately pressed to work. I also had my degree from Southern, and I figured that like most fairly well-known athletes, I wouldn't have a problem getting a job. Besides, in the back of my mind, I felt that I knew the game of basketball as well as anybody out there, and I could always hook up with a team as an assistant coach.

I guess I was naive, but I had no idea that making it off the court would be harder than the toughest hurdle I had encountered as a pro basketball player. I was about to face the biggest challenge of my life, one that I'd avoided since I was a child.

11

LIFE AFTER BASKETBALL

*Pro basketball, the dream that had motivated
me for all those years, was gone, seemingly
for good. And there was nothing to replace it.*

WHEN I RETIRED IN 1977, Betty, the kids, and I were living
in Bothell, a Seattle suburb. We had a beautiful four-
bedroom house, and standing on the front lawn you could
look out at Lake Washington. The Inglewood Country Club
was behind the house, and our backyard ended at the edge of
the 15th hole. It was a terrific spot, and that summer I spent a
lot of time at home playing with the kids and relaxing on the
golf course. I waited until the fall before I started making the
rounds looking for a job.

I started with restaurants and hotels, hoping to get some kind
of management trainee position where I could use my degree in
food and nutrition. Since I'd played for the Supersonics the previous year, I was fairly well known around the area. I didn't
have a problem getting interviews; nearly everybody I called
wanted to see me. But right from the start, a disappointing pat-
tern developed.

I'd show up with my diploma, and the personnel manager or
whoever conducted the interview would greet me with a great
big smile and handshake, then start telling me how much they
enjoyed watching me play basketball. Everything was fine as
long as we talked about the NBA and its players, particularly
stars like Rick Barry; Freddie Brown, who was the Sonics leading scorer; and Bill Russell, who had become a favorite as a
coach in Seattle. But the minute I brought up the subject of

work, the atmosphere changed. They immediately tightened up, and I could almost feel the chill in the room.

When talking about basketball, I was pretty relaxed myself, and my speech wasn't too bad. At least no one seemed to mind. But I tensed up when we got around to talking about a job. I was always nervous. I couldn't help it. When they asked what I wanted to do or how I thought I might fit into their company, I started stumbling over my words and stuttering. They'd just sit there, and I could see that look of surprise come over their faces. Most of them didn't know about my speech problem. They only knew that I'd played for the Sonics and had been an All-Star in the NBA. When they noticed how badly I spoke, I guess they were shocked. Usually, after about ten minutes, they'd pull out my résumé, take a long look at it, and say something like, "Well, Bob, you've had a great career, and we'd love to have you join our organization, *but* . . ."

There was always that *but*, and most interviews ended with them saying they didn't have anything that suited me at the time, *but* they would get back to me. They were always polite. And during the first month or so, I actually left a few of those offices thinking I had a shot at some kind of job. But after I'd been out there beating the pavement for three or four months and no one called, I realized that something was terribly wrong. I must have applied for forty or fifty jobs, and I didn't get one call from any of the people I saw.

A Disability, Not an Annoyance

Before long, I began to realize how much my success in sports had shielded me from the seriousness of my speech impediment. Suddenly, the chickens were coming home to roost, and no matter where I turned I couldn't avoid the problem.

It had always been there, but while playing in the NBA I ignored it most of the time. That fall, when I started thinking about the old days as a player, I wanted to kick myself. All of the jokes and embarrassing experiences I'd had came rushing back to mind. I thought about the times when my teammates teased me, when a few players snubbed me or tried to distance themselves from me when we were hanging out, when reporters walked into the locker room and ignored me after a game, or when I was forced into situations where I had to try to speak in front of big crowds.

One of the worst happened when my son Kevin asked me to take him to a father-son dinner sponsored by the Jaycees while I was still playing in Chicago. I always tried to duck situations like that because I knew somebody would try to have me get up and talk about the Bulls. But I wanted to be there with my son, so this time I had Betty call one of Kevin's teachers and make sure that I wouldn't have to speak. They agreed. That night, when I was introduced at the dinner, all the fathers and their kids stood up and started to cheer. They gave me a standing ovation. Then, somebody in the back of the room started yelling "Speech! Speech!" And before I knew what happened the whole crowd had joined him. They were all clapping and stomping and screaming, "Speech, speech!"

At first, I just sat in my chair, smiling and shaking my head no. Then the guy sitting next to me said, "Go on, Bob, just say a few words."

They practically dragged me up to the stage. When I got up there, my mind was running like a tape recorder on fast forward, but I couldn't get a single word out. The room was so quiet you could hear a pin drop—absolutely silent. And every eye was on me. I just froze. I must have stood there for three minutes without saying one word. Finally, I turned away and walked back to my seat. I just sat there with my head down while one of the teachers tried to make excuses for me. I hadn't been that ashamed and embarrassed since my school days in Bastrop.

127

I agonized over the incident for days. It really hurt me because it was not just me but also Kevin who was shamed by it. I felt as though I had let him down. Later I realized he was strong enough to deal with it, and he was proud of me anyway. Finally I put it aside. "The guy up at that podium was not Bob

Love," I told myself. I'd always been a positive person, and I didn't want to start pitying myself. I refused to let that incident hold me back.

Looking back on it, I know that I should have faced the problem then. I should have gotten some help. I did start out with a couple of speech therapists while I was in Chicago, but I never followed through on it, and after a few visits I'd drop out. Things were going well, and I'd always been able to excel despite stuttering. I didn't realize how radically things would change when I no longer played basketball. The whole thing came crashing down on me, and I quickly discovered that the inability to communicate was a disability, not just some annoying social problem.

Seeking Assistant Coaching Jobs

I did everything I could to find a job that fall and winter. I applied at all the places where I thought my degree might qualify me for work, and when that failed I started looking into jobs in basketball. I'd spent nearly twenty years of my life playing the game and learning everything I could about it. I felt that I knew as much as or more than many of the former players who were getting assistant coaching jobs. And I was convinced that I could make a contribution to an NBA team.

My friend Bill Russell had left the Supersonics, and after his assistant Bob Hopkins got off to a terrible start during the 1977–78 season, Lenny Wilkens was brought in as coach. Since I didn't know Lenny very well—he had always been a little distant with me—I didn't approach him or Seattle's management about a job. But I did start calling other teams and asking about assistant coaching jobs.

At that time there were only a few black coaches and almost no blacks at the management level in professional basketball. Bill Russell took over as player-coach of the Boston Celtics in 1966, and he was the first. Al Attles was hired by Golden State in 1970, and K. C. Jones coached the Bullets for three years before Dick Motta took over in 1976. Lenny Wilkens started as coach of the Portland Trail Blazers in 1974 before he moved to Seattle. And in 1977, the year I began looking for a job, the New York Knicks hired Willis Reed, and Elgin Baylor took over as coach of the New Orleans Jazz. Except for Zelmo Beaty, who coached the ABA's Virginia Squires for a few games at the end of the 1975–76 season, that was it.

Things were starting to change, but for the most part the coaching spots and executive positions went to white guys. I knew what the situation was when I started inquiring about a job—but I hoped that like Reed and Baylor, I could get in on what seemed like a breakthrough in accepting blacks in the coaching ranks during the mid-'70s.

When I look back on it now, I realize that the problem was that a lot of owners and coaches had bought into some old stereotypes about black athletes. To many of them, we were all "naturals"—they were willing to admit that we could *play* the game, but few gave us credit for being able to *think* about how it was played. Both inside and outside sports, the assumption was that blacks might be gifted artistically or athletically but they were incapable of leadership, thinking, and planning. It was the same bias that led a lot of people to believe blacks couldn't cut it as quarterbacks in professional football before the 1980s.

Even though there are still very few black executives or owners in the NBA, attitudes have changed a lot during the last twenty years. But in the late '70s, when I was searching for a job, the bias that Jimmy the Greek later infamously expressed was still very much a part of the game, and although I didn't want to admit it, I was suffering from a double handicap. It didn't stop me from looking, but being black and a stutterer, there was really not much chance of my being hired as a coach.

Still, I pressed ahead, trying to do something that nobody thought I had a shot at doing. It wasn't the first time, and I wasn't about to change my style. I approached a lot of teams during the next few years, and I'm sure I annoyed a lot of people—friends and guys that I'd never been that close to.

129

A few years later I even asked Dick Motta, who was coaching the Sacramento Kings at the time, for help. I called him when the team came into town to play Seattle, and we arranged to meet after the game.

As I said earlier, Motta and I had a strained relationship back in Chicago. But I still felt that he knew how hard I'd worked as a player, and despite our differences I thought he respected my knowledge of the game. I also knew that he had helped a couple of my teammates, Jerry Sloan and Bob Weiss, get jobs as assistant coaches.

When we met, I let him know that I needed a job and that I was interested in getting into coaching. I told him that I knew they had all the X-and-O guys they needed. But I felt that I could help his team by working with players on the court, showing them some of the moves and tricks that Oscar Robertson had passed on to me. Then after a little more small talk, I just came out and said, "Look, Dick, if you'd give me a chance, I think I'd be a real good assistant coach. I'm not the kind of guy who wants to draw up game plans, but every team needs someone who really knows how to play the game, a guy who can point out little things that opposing players are doing on offense or defense, show players how to take advantage of their opponents' weaknesses. I think I can do that. In fact, I know I can."

He hemmed and hawed, all the time smiling and trying to change the subject. Finally, he said, "Bob, I'll think about it. I'll let you know."

We talked for a little while longer, and, when he got up to leave, he said, "Don't worry, I'll get back to you Bob. I'll get back to you on it." I still haven't heard from him, but I'll never forget his reaction.

After that incident, I was mad as hell. I guess in the back of my mind, I felt that Motta owed me something. During the 1974–75 season, I had led Chicago on defense and offense, helping him get the Coach of the Year award. And for the seven full years I had played under him, I'd led the team in scoring. So for a while when I was struggling and out of work in the late '70s, I gave in to some of the bitterness that was building up. I just

130

couldn't see the whole picture. I kept thinking that Motta had hired Jerry Sloan, even though he had no experience. He had given Bobby Weiss and Matt Goukas a shot, but he didn't even have the courtesy to call me back. I was frustrated and angry, and, for the first time in my life, I started feeling sorry for myself.

During that period I also contacted Bobby Weiss, who was with the San Antonio Spurs, and asked if he had a spot open for an assistant coach. He flat-out told me that he couldn't hire me because I didn't have any experience. I had nearly reached the end of my rope by then, and I exploded.

"Look, Bobby," I said, "I know more about the game than you do. I was a better player than you, and I can do everything that any other coach in the league does."

He just looked at me and calmly said, "You still don't have any experience. I can't hire you."

That was the response I got nearly every time I approached someone about coaching. And after a while, although I still hoped that I'd get back into basketball, I stopped asking. I was getting down on myself, and I was angry at a lot of the guys I'd known or played with in the NBA. But I really didn't want it to appear as though I were begging for a job.

It took some time for me to get over that experience, and I still think that if one of them had have given me an opportunity as a coach I would have risen to the challenge. But a few years later, I began to understand their reasons for hesitating to hire me. It wasn't just a racial thing, it was also my speaking problem. And when I eventually confronted that disability, I began to see how much it had affected the way other people looked at me.

131

Odd Jobs

Of course, I didn't have that insight while I was struggling to find work. During that time, I was getting more and more desperate. It was rough, but I got through it by turning to friends, guys that I'd met who either owned businesses or had positions with companies that allowed them to put a word in for me. It was hectic, and sometimes I was forced to swallow my pride and accept anything that was offered. It also meant I had to spend a lot of time away from Seattle, Betty, and our children, since some of the work was in Chicago, where I'd played for most of my career.

We were just scraping by, so I was scrambling, trying to make ends meet. And although I was hoping to find a trainee position that would allow me to use my college degree, I had to take a lot of dead-end jobs. I couldn't afford to sit around and wait. I think I must have done about every awful, low-level job that anybody could imagine during those years. I dug ditches for a construction gang, delivered food for a catering company, worked in bars and restaurants doing everything from cooking and serving drinks to cleaning up and washing dishes, and for a while worked as a recruiter at Malcolm X College in Chicago.

It was frustrating, and I was scared of going under. I just couldn't see a way out of the rut. I was in limbo, lost, with no real direction—just scurrying around like a chicken with its head cut off.

I didn't know where I was going, and all I could do was keep running, struggling, and trying to keep up. I didn't have time to think about anything else. Pro basketball, the dream that had motivated me for all those years, was gone, seemingly for good. And there was nothing to replace it. I'd read and heard about athletes who had been at the top and, after they'd stopped playing, ended up on skid row or worse. I'd even seen some ballplayers, friends of mine, who had it all—the finest homes, clothes, and women—and still fell apart and hit rock bottom. We've all read about the guys who, when the slightest thing went wrong, gave in to drugs or crime or beat their wives or ended up in jail. I thank God that I was able to resist those things.

In a way, I was lucky. But I think it was the influence of my grandmother that really saved me. The lessons she drilled into my head about not being ashamed of hard work and never giving up had stuck with me. And whenever I really faltered and felt like throwing in the towel, I thought of the way she struggled to feed our family and how much dignity she had even when she was forced to do the dirtiest jobs out there. It was almost like she was looking over my shoulder, repeating the words I'd heard so many times before, "It's up to you, son. You got to do it for yourself." And if I hadn't listened to her voice, if I hadn't somehow found the strength, I could have easily fallen by the wayside.

Trouble at Home

As it was, the situation took its toll. It was during that time that my marriage to Betty started falling apart. I couldn't get a good job because of my stuttering, I was barely able to support our family, and I didn't know where to turn. Betty was upset. Rightfully so, I guess. And the longer it went on, the more tense things became. After a while I started hanging out at bars in Seattle just to get away from home. We were drifting apart, and whenever a job opportunity came up in Chicago I jumped at it. I always took care of the bills and my kids, but the relationship had become so strained that, more and more, I needed to get away.

It was during that time that I made the biggest mistake I ever made in my life. I had met a woman in Chicago back in 1974, while I was still playing with the Bulls. Her name was Denise Bouldin, and she had been a counselor at the Dr. Martin Luther King Boys Club when I played in their summer league. We ran into each other a few times afterward and became friends. Then when things started going bad at home, we started hanging out together.

At the time, Denise lived in the Rockwell Gardens projects at Western and Adams. It was a low-income, drug- and gang-infested complex, and Denise was anxious to get out of there. She was an intelligent, high-strung, ambitious woman, and she looked just like a movie star. When I first saw her, she reminded me of a dark-skinned Lena Horne. She was tall, about 5 feet

8 inches, and had run track and trained for a while as a gymnast. She had a perfectly toned, graceful body. She also had smooth skin, keen features, and a knockout smile. Denise was beautiful. She knew it, and so did everybody else who met her.

As things got worse at home, my relationship with Denise heated up. And by the early '80s we were seeing a lot of each other. Betty was back in Seattle while I worked at Malcolm X College, and I was spending as much time as I could with Denise. Even after I returned to Seattle, I still found excuses for going to Chicago. Then, in 1982, Denise moved to the West Coast and enrolled in the Seattle police academy. And although we usually didn't get together in public, I continued seeing her.

I really didn't know where the relationship was going, but I was becoming more and more attached to her. I was depressed, frustrated with not being able to find a good job, and unsure of my future. With everything else falling apart, Denise seemed like one of the best things that had ever happened to me. I guess I was drawing on her energy and drive to keep myself going. At the time, just being around her made me feel better about myself.

She was a stunning woman who was smart and ambitious. Unfortunately, as I'd discover later, she was much more ambitious than I imagined.

12

NO FAITH IN MY FUTURE

*Finally, I stumbled into my bedroom and got
on my knees. I prayed to the Lord to give me
strength, to give me courage to go on.*

LESS THAN A YEAR AFTER DENISE arrived in Seattle, Betty filed
for a divorce. And strange as it may seem, the whole thing
caught me by surprise.

See, I had never intended to leave my wife and kids. I was in
a daze during that time, stumbling around looking for some way
to put my life back together. I had no direction, no plan. In fact,
I was barely aware of what I was doing. I'd been cut off from
the only thing I really knew how to do—play basketball. And
since I couldn't find a good job and was suddenly faced with the
reality of my speech problem, I felt totally inadequate. Still, the
last thing I wanted was to be separated from my family.

Betty and I really had a very good relationship, and I think
our problems could have been rectified if she hadn't filed for
divorce. Like I said, though, I was out there. My life seemed
totally out of control. No one would hire me. I was running the
streets, trying to find my way, just running from place to place.
And there was no communication between Betty and me.

I was ashamed, and I should have gone to her, faced the problems, and talked things out. I didn't, and she didn't initiate anything, either. She didn't grab me and say, "Bob, hey, let's do this
or you should do that." I was desperate and really needed guidance, but no one was there. At that time, I don't even think that
Betty knew about Denise. But she had started listening to all of
her friends, and she knew that I was running the streets, hang-

ing out in bars and clubs. Her friends told her they saw me at this place or that place—that I was talking to this person and that person. She was fed up, and I guess she didn't have any more faith in my future than I did at the time.

Still, it was ultimately my fault. I'd been strong enough to resist the total collapse that some people go through when they take a big fall and find themselves at the bottom of the heap, but I wasn't strong enough to resist the temptation of going outside my family for support. Afterward I had a lot of regrets, and I tried to talk to Betty. But once her lawyers filed the papers, it was too late. She had made up her mind.

Betty and I got a divorce in 1983, and a month or so later I moved in with Denise. At first we lived alone, but later we shared an apartment with her brother Pete in Kirkland, a suburb of Seattle. Although I missed being with my children, Denise and I got along very well during that time. We both loved Chicago, and when we could find the time, we went back there together. Those few months during the fall of 1983 were really the best times we spent together. I was struggling, looking for a steady job, but there was money coming in from deferred NBA payments and my health was good. That's when Denise and I decided to get married.

We were married in Chicago, and after the wedding we returned to Kirkland. Denise was really supportive when we got back, and despite being separated from my children most of the time, I was beginning to come out of my funk. I had a chance to start over with Denise, and I wanted to put the past behind me, forget about basketball, and get on with my life. I was still depressed, but for the first time in years I felt good about bucking the odds and, no matter what it took, beginning a new career.

136

Back Surgery Redux

Then just after we returned, my back and legs started really acting up. I'd had some pain since I quit basketball, but I'd ignored it. It was way down on the list when compared to the other problems I'd had over the past six years. It was a lot easier than playing through pain in the NBA, and after a while I just accepted it as something I had to live with. But a couple of months after I returned, the pain had become unbearable. There were days when I could hardly walk. I fought through it for weeks, then I decided I'd better see someone. My medical records were still in Chicago, so in August 1983 I called the doctor I'd seen when I was with the Bulls and arranged for an examination. I left for Chicago two days later.

By that time I knew something was seriously wrong with my back. And after the examination, I found that it was much more severe than I had thought. A week after arriving in Chicago, the doctors said I had to have an operation immediately, that with any further delay I'd risk permanent injury to my spine. Despite the previous operation, the disc injury that I'd sustained back in 1966 had gotten worse. They referred me to a specialist in Los Angeles who was an expert in delicate back surgery.

It was a huge disappointment for me. I'd just remarried and was starting to focus on beginning a new life, and suddenly there was another setback. When I called and told Denise, although she was concerned, she didn't seem too disturbed by the news. She assured me that she was in my corner and that everything would be all right. I went to Los Angeles and stayed with my mother.

My back surgery was scheduled immediately, and Denise flew down to Los Angeles to be with me. The long, three-hour operation was a success. Afterward, they told me that I was truly lucky. Essentially, they had to redo the operation that had been done in 1966. Twenty years of twisting and leaping and sprinting back and forth on hardwood floors had taken its toll; and, of course, my delaying the surgery hadn't helped. I'd narrowly escaped permanent disability. If I'd waited even a month longer, the damage to my spine would have been irreversible.

As it was, the doctors said that after surgery I'd probably never be able to walk again without a cane or crutches. That prognosis scared me a little, but even at the moment I first heard it there was a part of me that didn't accept it. In the past, whenever somebody told me I couldn't do something, I just ignored it and tried harder. And I kept telling myself that this wasn't much different.

When I awoke after the operation, Denise and my mother were in the room. They were both happy to see that I was OK. But a few days later, when Denise discovered that I *might* have to walk with a cane, she was visibly upset. She got real quiet. It was like someone had let the air out of a balloon. Finally, she stammered out something like, "You're going to be a cripple. . . ." Then while my mother tried to encourage me, she stood there as if she was in shock. After I assured her that I would prove the doctor wrong, she seemed to pull herself together. She stayed until the next day, then went back to Seattle and returned to work.

Growing Suspicions

During the next few weeks, I kept trying to get in touch with Denise in Seattle. We had only spent a few months together since being married, and I was anxious to see her. But nearly every time I called, she was gone. Didn't matter what time of the day or night, she'd be out. She had passed the exam and started her job as a rookie police officer a month or so before our wedding. And whenever I did catch her at home, she'd complain about the odd hours and long tours of duty and insist that her work was keeping her busy. Still, I was getting a little suspicious. I had a feeling that something was going on, but I really didn't want to deal with it. I was focused on getting well as quickly as I could. And even while I was flat on my back in Los Angeles, I never doubted it. I knew that I'd never stop trying to recover completely.

Being at my mother's house in Watts helped. Baba had passed, but I got along very well with my brothers and sisters.

My mom took real good care of me and made sure I was comfortable while I recuperated. It was also exceptionally warm that year. It was winter, but I was able to get out nearly every day and at least hobble around the neighborhood on my crutches. Soon I was getting around pretty good, so I called Denise and told her that I was thinking about coming back to Seattle. I knew I couldn't lie around my mother's house forever, and I wanted to get back to see my kids and be with Denise.

Denise kept hesitating, though, trying to put it off. Whenever I brought it up, she'd say, "Maybe you should stay down there a little longer, honey. You're not well enough to come back yet. You don't want to rush things, and, you know, I won't have time to take care of you like your mother can." She also suggested that since I didn't have any income, I should apply for disability. The Rockwell Gardens projects where she was raised was one of the roughest, poorest sections in Chicago, and growing up she had learned how to grab whatever she could get. I think she was more afraid of poverty than anything else. So when it came to money, she was always on the case. I took her advice and filled out the application forms.

Finally, in March I decided to return to Seattle. I had to find out what was going on. I still had this old raggedy car, a 1965 blue Oldsmobile that my friend Jim Maryland had sold to me for a dollar back in Chicago. He'd had the car stored away for about fifteen years. When he opened the garage door, it was covered with dust and spiderwebs; rats came running out the door. He laughed and said, "Don't worry, it runs well, that's what counts." Jim was right. It had gotten me safely from Chicago to Los Angeles, and although it didn't last long afterward, it survived the drive up the coast to Seattle without any problems.

I was still on crutches and could barely get around when I arrived in Kirkland. And just as I thought, Denise was gone most of the time. She always had something to do and some excuse for being out all hours of the night. I didn't want to deal with it, but after I'd been home for a couple of months I was almost certain that Denise was seeing someone. She was a beautiful woman, and I knew that guys were always flirting with her, telling her how pretty she was, and asking her out. Still, when she stayed out until two or three in the morning, she would come in and say that she'd been working or partying with her girlfriends. I wanted to believe her, so I didn't question her or argue about it. I didn't want to confront her unless I was sure that she was cheating.

I'd met some of her friends from the police department. And one of them, Angie, was married with a few kids. She was a cop, but she seemed like a real homebody. The three of us were at a bar one evening, and when Denise went to the ladies' room, I decided to ask Angie about Denise.

I just blurted out the question: "Hey, Angie, do you know what's happening with Denise? She stays out all times of the night, goes out of town for days on police work. I know she talks to you—what's going on?"

She never answered me, just looked away and shook her head. Didn't say a word, but I could tell by the look on her face that she was protecting Denise. Still, I didn't do anything about it. I just tried to blot it out and ignore it.

That wasn't always easy. I'd met and developed a friendship with this bunch of guys who hung out at the Appointment, a bar and restaurant in downtown Seattle that was owned by a friend of mine. And about that time, I noticed that the guys would start laughing and jiving about "do right women" whenever I came into the bar. Finally, one said, "Damn, man! Don't you know about Ernie, the married guy who's trying to steal your wife?" I was as surprised as I was embarrassed. It seemed as though everybody knew what was going on between Denise and me. My business was all over the street.

140

Still, at the time I felt that all I could do was let it pass. I was trying to settle all this other stuff, struggling to recover from the surgery, thinking about how to find work and get my life together. Maybe I was just hoping that if I ignored it the problem would go away, but I convinced myself that it wasn't the time to confront Denise.

Money Changes Everything

As it turned out, the situation quickly got out of hand. Circumstances forced me to do something. It started with a check that I received from the government. It was a retroactive lumpsum disability payment for a few thousand. I showed it to Denise, then just put it into a bureau drawer. I figured I'd deposit it the next time I went to the bank. A day or so later, another check came. This one was for $30,000 and came from the Chicago Bulls; it was deferred salary payment from my last contract. I was as surprised as I was happy. Despite our problems, I wanted to show it to Denise. But she came in late that evening and I didn't have a chance to say anything. The very next day, a third check arrived. This one was for about $25,000 and was also from the Bulls. Suddenly, it seemed that my luck was changing, that everything was turning around. And I guess that somewhere in the back of my mind, I was hoping that if I started bringing in some money and got back on my feet, well, maybe it would help me patch things up with Denise.

When I showed her the checks, she grabbed me and gave me this big hug. I don't think she had ever seen that much money in her life. It was like the old days. I hadn't seen her that happy and excited since I'd first met her when she lived in the projects. I asked her to take me to the bank that afternoon but she said she had something else to do—there would be plenty of time tomorrow. That was fine by me. I put all the checks in one of my suit jacket pockets and hung it in the closet.

The next morning, Denise got up really early. In fact, when I woke up, she was gone. I didn't hear her get up or leave because we'd been up late celebrating the night before and my back was bothering me. I completely forgot about the checks that day. But the following afternoon, when I went into the closet and checked my suit, the pockets were empty.

When Denise came home from work, I immediately asked her if she'd moved the checks. She said, "Yeah, Bob, I put them in the bank. Don't worry, I've got them in a safe place. I'll take care of them."

"How did you do that?" I asked. "I never signed them."

"That's all right, baby, I signed them for you," she said.

I didn't know what she was up to, but I was disturbed. I told her she should have let me sign my own checks. It was my money. She shrugged it off, saying, "Don't worry, I took care of the money. Everything's all right."

I didn't say anything else about it for a few days, but I was still concerned. And about a week later, I told her I wanted to know exactly where my money was; I asked to see the deposit slip. She told me she didn't have the slip but the checks had been deposited in the Old National Bank, which was downtown on Third Avenue. Since I didn't have an account at that bank, I became even more suspicious. I didn't say anything to Denise, but that afternoon I took the bus downtown and went to Old National.

I'm not sure if it was just the sight of a very tall black man hobbling in on a cane or if somehow Denise had warned them, but from the moment I walked in, the bank managers and tellers seemed to be on edge. Of course, it could have just been my attitude—I was determined to find out about my checks and was so tense that the veins must have been bulging in my forehead. I'm sure they could see how agitated I was. When I finally got to see a manager, I asked if my wife had deposited a large sum of money in the bank. She checked, then came back and said, "Yes, she made a deposit in her account."

"Eh, eh . . . in . . . *her* account," I stammered. I was visibly disturbed, and without noticing it I'd begun tapping my cane against the side of her desk. When she stared down at the cane, I stopped. She tried to assure me that it wasn't unusual for a wife to put money into her own account, but I demanded to see copies of the checks. By then, the manager was getting a little nervous. I think she was afraid of what I might do next. Anyway, she got up and brought back the copies.

It was amazing. Denise had done a fairly good job of imitating my signature. Staring at the checks, I started thinking about this guy she had been hanging out with. And the more I thought about it, the angrier I got.

I was upset and hurt, so I was stuttering badly, and it took me a few minutes to make the manager understand that I had not given Denise permission to cash my checks.

"Th-this is not m-my si-sig . . . nature," I finally stammered. "I want m-my mo-money."

"Sorry," she said, "but there's nothing we can do about that. She's your wife."

I sat there struggling to find words, trying to tell her what was going on with me and Denise—why I would have never allowed my wife to put my money in her account. The more I stumbled over the words, the more frustrated and agitated I got. Before I knew it, my voice had risen. I was shouting and stammering, and everybody was staring at us. That's when the manager pushed her chair back from the desk. She was trying to act normal, but her eyes were as wide as silver dollars. After a few minutes, she stood up and backed away. Speaking very slowly, as if she were talking to an unruly child, she told me that if I didn't calm down and stop all the clamor, she'd have to ask me to leave or call the police. The bank's security guard had already started moving toward us.

"Oh—ok," I said, "but wha . . . what can I . . . do?"

"Well, you can file forgery charges against her," she said.

I thought about that for a few minutes. Bringing charges against Denise had never entered my mind; all I wanted was to get my money back. Then I thought, what the hell, maybe it would help persuade her to be more cooperative. After the manager gave me the papers, I quietly left the bank. Everyone seemed relieved.

At home that evening, I asked Denise for my money again. "I don't have your money," she yelled, "you know it's in the bank. Why do you keep bothering me about it?" This time, she stormed into the bedroom and slammed the door behind her.

I thought about following her, pressing things, but I was so mad I didn't know what would have happened. Instead, I walked out. I caught the first bus that came along, didn't care where it was going. I stayed on that bus for hours, riding and thinking; and, the more I thought, the hotter I got. When I

143

finally returned home, I was ready for a confrontation. I rushed into the bedroom but Denise was gone. So were a lot of her personal belongings. It didn't take much imagination to see that she was getting ready to leave me. Now I was really incensed. My wife had not only taken all my money, she was getting ready to walk out on me. When I finally went to bed I tossed and turned all night, couldn't sleep a wink.

Denise didn't return that night.

A Second Divorce Looms

I had a doctor's appointment the next day. But before leaving home that morning, I filled out the forms that I'd gotten from the bank. I dropped them off at the police station on the way to the doctor's office. By the time I returned home, it was late afternoon. And even before I opened the door, I had a strange feeling that something was wrong. Still, when I stepped inside I was shocked.

Nearly everything in the house was gone. All of her clothes and personal things, the television and most of the furniture, all the jewelry and trophies, and what little cash that was left had disappeared. The house had been cleaned out—emptied except for my clothes, a few large pieces of furniture, and the things she'd left in her brother's room.

On the living room floor, she had left a note. It read: *I didn't want to be married to a guy who couldn't speak and I definitely don't want to be married to a guy who's going to be a cripple for the rest of his life.*

After I read the note, I just slumped to the floor—sat there for hours. I was devastated. I had never been hurt that badly. Finally, I stumbled into my bedroom and got on my knees. I prayed to the Lord to give me strength, to give me courage to go on. Afterward, I sprawled across the bed, exhausted and numb. At least she had left something for me to sleep on.

13

YOU GOT TO DO IT YOURSELF

Still, whenever it seemed that I'd
reconciled myself to giving in, I'd hear my
grandmother's voice in the background.
Ain't nobody out here that's perfect, son—you
got to have a dream. You got to do it yourself.

MUST HAVE STAYED LOCKED AWAY in that apartment for over
a week. I'm not sure now how long it was; it all seems like a
blur. But I remember feeling paralyzed and broken—and it
wasn't just my back and the physical pain I was in. I was almost
ready to give up. Denise's brother came in and out, and there
were a couple of calls from Betty, but it seemed as if I were in
a dream. I ignored everything around me. I know I must have
eaten and wandered around the house, but I don't remember
much of it. But I do clearly remember lying in my bed in that
bare room and just staring up at the ceiling. I felt empty and
useless. It seemed as if there was nowhere to turn. I couldn't
move, couldn't even work up the energy to think about what to
do next.

Then, about ten days after I'd filed the complaint against
Denise, I received a call from the Seattle police department asking if I had filed a forgery claim. I said yes, and the officer on
the phone said, "That's your wife, isn't it?"

I was still furious about my money, and in one broken burst,
I shouted, "So what. I didn't tell her to sign those checks. I
don't have a dime—not one cent."

"Look," he said, "your wife told us you gave her permission
to cash those checks. You know it's your word against hers."

After that I began stammering, tripping over my words, getting madder by the second, and I couldn't get a single word out. All I did was stutter and gasp for breath. Exasperated, the cop finally shouted, "Don't call the station again—we can't accept this claim," and slammed the receiver down.

When he hung up on me, I was devastated. I had the feeling that if I pressed the issue the police would start investigating me. I felt helpless, absolutely powerless—everything and everybody seemed to have turned against me. I had never faced anything like that before. There had been bad times when I was a kid, but I'd always had athletics to fall back on. Those days were gone. There was nothing to fall back on, no safety net.

I was still hobbling around, barely able to walk. There was no money. I had no job, no wife, no future—nothing. I was scared, hurt, and furious. Desperate, I decided that I had to find Denise and try convincing her to at least return some of my money. I knew the chances were slim, but I had to do something. And if nothing else, the thought of confronting Denise gave me the energy to get up and get out of that apartment.

Confronting Denise

I didn't know where she had gone or where she moved her things, but I'd heard that she and her boyfriend Ernie hung out at an after-hours joint in downtown Seattle. When the other bars around the city closed for the night, at about one o'clock, that was where all the brothers and sisters gathered. It stayed open until the wee hours of the morning. I couldn't think of any other place where I might find her. I decided to try it that night.

I took the bus down there and hobbled in on my cane. I arrived early, around eleven o'clock, and found a spot off to the side in a dark corner where I thought nobody would see me. I wasn't sure what I was going to do, and as I sat there I began fidgeting and sweating. My heart was racing but my eyes were pinned on the door. At first, only a few people wandered in— the place was dead. It was after one o'clock when a crowd started gathering and the DJ pumped up the music. By then, I'd had a few drinks. It wasn't long before Denise and her little friend came strutting through the door.

The first thing I noticed was that she had a new mink stole around her neck—I couldn't help thinking that a couple thousand dollars of my money must have gone for that. She was stunning. Dressed to kill in a short black dress and these real high-heeled shoes. Ernie was right behind her. He was only about 5 feet 6 inches, so wearing heels she towered over him. He must have been twice her age, in his 60s, but he had this little boy's smile on his face. It was almost like I could read his mind. Seemed like he was thinking, *Damn, nobody is gonna believe this, but here I am with the prettiest woman in Seattle.* And Denise was switching through there like she was on stage—knew she looked good and everybody was watching. I almost got up and walked over to them as soon as they came in, but I thought, *Naw, I'm gonna sit here and see what happens.*

About ten minutes later, and it's the last thing I remember clearly, a Jackie Wilson song came on—one of those old, funky, bluesy tunes about "dogging me around." That's when Denise and her friend stepped out onto the dance floor. She put her arms around his neck, and they started to slow dance, grinding like they were making love out there. When I saw that, the blood rushed to my head. I just snapped—couldn't control myself. I scrambled up from the table and limped out toward them. I didn't even notice the other dancers—just pushed past them as if they weren't even there. It was almost like I was possessed or dreaming. When I got close, I lifted the cane and started to swing.

Just then, Denise saw me. "Bob! No, don't hit me!" she shouted.

I lunged toward her and swung the cane wildly. Denise ducked, then pulled away from Ernie and stepped back. Ernie ducked as I swung again. Thank God, I missed them—didn't hit a thing but air. As I stumbled and tried to regain my balance, a woman standing nearby screamed and the crowd scattered.

Denise turned and ran toward the door, and Ernie scrambled out behind her. It must have looked like a scene from some slapstick comedy routine, but I went limping and hopping after them, waving the cane in the air.

I couldn't keep up with them, and by the time I got outside Ernie was standing beside his car waiting. I thought he'd gone to get his pistol, because his hand was in his outside jacket pocket like he was holding something, so I stopped about fifteen feet from the car. It was a dangerous situation, but I was too mad to care.

I said, "Er . . . Er, ah, Ernie." I was nervous and stuttering, barely able to get a sound out. Then I just blurted out, "Man . . . le-let me . . . sp-speak . . . to you." It took some time, but I was finally able to tell him, "This is my wife, man. She took all the money I had in the world. Why don't you let her alone until we get a divorce?"

He looked up at me, cold as hell, and said, "I ain't got nothing to do with that, man. That's something you have to settle with her. But don't ever come at me like that again."

I guess God or my grandmother or somebody was looking out for me that night, because he kept his hand in his pocket. I was enraged, but there was nothing I could do. When Denise walked over and grabbed his arm, I just shook my head. I backed off, turned around, and hobbled away from them. I could hear Denise laughing, and Ernie shouted, "Fuck you, you goddamn cripple."

It was a half-mile trek to the bus stop; and, limping away from Denise's laughter, it seemed like the longest walk I'd ever taken. I caught the last bus and slumped down into a seat. I can't remember what I was thinking during the ride home. I do know that my stomach was in knots, and I was too frustrated and embarrassed to even look at the driver.

It would be months before I saw Denise again, and I never got my money back. She filed for a separation after that night, and about a year later we got a divorce. During the court hearings, the judge stipulated that if my trophies, gold chains, and All-Star rings were ever found they had to be returned to me. It was a nice gesture, but I never saw them again either.

148

Whatever Is Necessary to Survive

Meanwhile, my life had hit rock bottom. Everything had gone wrong. I was alone, broke, still unable to walk without the cane, and without any prospects for a job. At first, I really didn't know what to do, which way to turn. I just marked time—thought about trying to survive on my disability checks. Then a few weeks later I put the cane away and forced myself to try walking without it. At first I stayed in the house, taking little gimpy steps and moving real slow. Then I tried walking outside. And before long I was strong enough to go downtown, walk around without the cane, and take a bus back home.

As I gradually got my strength back, I began realizing I was lucky that I hadn't been hurt when I confronted Denise and Ernie. It was foolish; anything could have happened out in that parking lot. I could have been killed, and he had every right to protect himself in that situation. I was also glad that I hadn't hit them. If I had followed through on my first instinct, done something to harm them, I could have ended up in jail. I didn't get my money back, and I was literally still struggling to get back on my feet, but at least I had a chance to pull myself up and move on.

Still, I was broke, and, although it was uncomfortable staying with Denise's brother Pete, I couldn't afford to move out of the Kirkland apartment. On top of that, I realized that I'd fallen behind on my child support payments for my ex-wife Betty and my children. The disability checks weren't enough. I was desperate, and I knew I had to find a way to support my family—at least make sure they had enough food. That's when I asked Betty to go down to the welfare office and apply for relief. Of course, she refused.

"I'm not going down there," she said. "I'm not gonna let those people see me in the welfare office. These are your kids, you go. You apply for welfare. I'm not going."

I knew Betty would object even before I asked, and I would have done it myself except that I was still having a hard time getting around. Finally, I didn't have a choice. I went to the welfare office and applied for food stamps. Since I was on disability and unable to work, I got them immediately. Every month I took a bus to the welfare office and picked up the food stamps. They were for Betty and the kids, so the first time I got them I gave them to her so she could go up to the store and buy groceries.

"Forget it," she said. "I'm never going to the supermarket with food stamps. I won't let anybody see me using food stamps."

Betty and I had lived comfortably for most of our marriage, and for her, welfare, food stamps, anything that smacked of poverty was a comedown. She didn't want to deal with it. Even though she had lost the house in Bothell about six months after our divorce, she was a proud woman who was trying to keep up appearances. By that time, I'd begun to realize that some concessions had to be made. Things weren't going to be the way they were—at least not in the near future. I'd grown up poor, and, if nothing else, it had taught me that sometimes you have to do whatever is necessary to survive. I knew I had to try to support my kids, keep them from going hungry, and if it meant using food stamps, so be it. I wasn't embarrassed or ashamed.

My old car had broken down and it still hadn't been repaired, so I tried to get Betty to drive me to the supermarket, wait outside, then give me a ride back to her place. But she didn't want anything to do with it, and she refused. She was living in Belleview at the time, and the nearest mall was about a mile and a half away from her house. Whenever I couldn't get a friend to drive me out there from Kirkland, I'd take a bus that dropped me off near the mall.

I did the shopping, then loaded six or seven bags of groceries into a shopping cart, and pushed it out to the highway at the end of the parking lot. It was almost impossible to find a taxi in that part of the city, and there was no bus that went anywhere near Betty's house. So when I didn't have a ride, I had to haul those groceries on foot.

It was impossible to carry all the bags at the same time, so I'd take them across the street two or three at a time. Then I'd take a couple of bags and walk maybe fifty yards down the road, put them down, and go back for a couple more. I was like a one-man-relay team. I had to keep retracing my steps, going back to get two or three bags, then setting them down and doubling back to get the others. It was rough since I'd just gotten to the point where I could even walk without a cane. Then too, I was always worried about someone driving up and taking the bags that I'd left behind. On those days when I couldn't get a ride, it took more than an hour to lug that food from the market to Betty's house.

I knew I looked foolish as hell walking back and forth carrying all those bags up the road. People driving by would sometimes slow down and watch with amazement; they must have thought I was crazy. But no one ever stopped to give me a lift. I was so exhausted when I got the groceries to the house, and I'd plop down in a chair and try to catch my breath. Of course, that's when Betty would rush into the kitchen to see what I'd brought. It wasn't easy for me or my family, but we survived. And, if I had to do the same thing again today, I wouldn't hesitate.

A New Start at Nordstrom

The end of 1984 was one of the most critical times in my life. I had been sitting around living off disability checks and food stamps for a few months, and despite being able to move around without a cane, I was feeling sorry for myself. By then, I realized that with my speech problem I'd never get the kind of job I'd been searching for. I was spending a lot of time in bars, having a few beers and hanging out with the fellows and drinking, and I was really tempted to give it up, quit fighting and just sit back and let the government take care of me. I was on the ropes, more depressed than I'd been in my entire life.

Still, whenever it seemed that I'd reconciled myself to giving in, I'd hear my grandmother's voice in the background. *Ain't nobody out here that's perfect, son—you got to have a dream. You got to do it yourself.* Then one morning when I awoke, something inside me snapped. Lying in bed, groggy and fuzzy eyed, I realized that I couldn't go on that way. I had to get out of the rut that I'd fallen into.

That's when I made a decision to start over. I knew I had to do something to change my life. Even if I couldn't get the kind of job I wanted, I had to find work. That afternoon, I bought the newspaper and started looking in the want ads. One of the first ads I saw was for a job at Nordstrom, a well-known department store, which was downtown on the corner of Pike and Fourth Avenue. Any high school dropout could have done the jobs they were offering, but that didn't bother me. I called Richard Frame, a friend who worked at the store, and he said he would take me in and introduce me to one of the managers.

The next day, I met the black store manager, Jim Nicholson, and filled out an application. I told him that I was willing to start anywhere, as long as there was a chance for advancement if I did a good job. Like most of the people I'd interviewed with, he was skeptical at first. He knew I'd been an NBA ballplayer, and he wondered why I was applying for such a low-level job. I just flat-out told him that I was desperate and I needed work. A day or so later, someone from the personnel department called and offered me a job in their restaurant division. And on December 28, 1984, I began working in the cafeteria at Nordstrom. I was making $4.45 an hour washing dishes and bussing tables.

It was the most embarrassing, humiliating work I'd ever done. I'd had worse jobs, of course. As a teenager in Bastrop, I'd picked cotton with the rest of the black folks, and after I left the NBA I'd scrubbed floors and emptied garbage and whatnot; but those jobs had been with little catering companies where I worked behind the scenes or at night when nobody was around. Nordstrom was a huge department store, and practically everybody who came through Seattle stopped in there. People who had seen me playing in the NBA came in, and a few times ballplayers who were in town to play the Sonics stopped at the cafeteria.

152

I'd hear them mumbling under their breath, "Hey, man, that's Bob Love. That guy used to be great. Look at him now, cleaning tables and picking up dirty dishes. What happened? He was bad!" Kids would see me and their parents would point and whisper, "See, that's what happens to them big-time sports folks when they finish. That's a real shame . . . he used to have it all."

Usually, I'd try to ignore the comments. But sometimes when ballplayers came in, I'd go over to their table, smile, and say, "How you doing?" I'd pretend that everything was fine, that it was just another job. It meant that I had to eat my pride, but I couldn't let other people's opinions affect me. It wasn't easy, and sometimes I couldn't face it. Many a day, when I was finished working I'd hang around the kitchen until the restaurant closed in order to avoid running into other employees who got off at the same time.

See, I took a bus to work every day, and the bus stop was right in front of the Mayflower Hotel and Restaurant, which was across the street from Nordstrom. A lot of times after work, I'd go into the hotel bar to have a beer while I waited for the bus. It was a hangout for Nordstrom employees, and all these black guys, managers and salesmen, would come in there wearing suits and ties. Dressed back, you know. They'd sit there laughing and talking about women and parties and what a great time they had the night before. Then I'd walk in wearing my soiled white shirt and pants, which were always covered with grit and grease and food stains from cleaning and washing dishes. Nearly every time I walked through the door, some guy at their table would start shouting, "Bob Love, Bob Love." Then they'd call the waitress or waiter and have them bring me a beer.

I'm sure they thought they were doing the right thing, but the last thing I wanted was having somebody call attention to who I was and letting everybody know how far I'd fallen. After they bought a drink for me, they usually started whispering among themselves. But it didn't matter; I could always tell when someone was talking about me. Still, I was always polite. I'd raise my glass and stammer out, "Hey, man, how you doing? I really do appreciate the beers—th-thanks."

When they asked if everything was all right, I'd say, "Yeah, man, everything's cool. I . . . I did fine today."

I never joined them. I just sat in the corner, drank my beer, and waited for the bus to arrive. It happened all the time. And though I learned to deal with it, I never got used to it. I was always anxious to get the hell out of there. I was embarrassed, but I kept telling myself that it didn't really matter. I wasn't going to be shamed out of finishing what I'd set out to do. I had a mission, a goal, and I was determined to see it through.

Hard Work Pays Off

Before long, despite those embarrassing moments, things started looking up for me. A few months after I began at Nordstrom I met Natalie, a city government employee who had come into my friend's bar to have a drink after work. She was a bright, articulate woman, and she seemed interested in me and sympathetic to my problems. We went out on a few dates and, within a month or so, I left the Kirkland apartment, which I'd been sharing with Denise's brother, and moved into her place in Seattle. Natalie was there for me during some of the roughest times at Nordstrom, and her support helped keep me going.

Then, about a year after I started working, John Nordstrom, one of the store owners, approached me. He told me he had talked to Jim Dickinson, the general manager of the restaurant division, who told him that I was an excellent worker. "We've noticed it also," he said. "We think you could have a future with our company, and we'd like to help you get your life together. But first, you'll have to do something about your speech. If you're willing to give it a try, we'll pay for it."

At first, I couldn't believe what he'd said. It was the opportunity I'd been waiting for. It seemed as though the weight of the world had been suddenly lifted from my shoulders. It had been years since anyone had shown that kind of personal interest in me. For the first time since I was a child and my grandmother had taken care of me, I felt that someone was concerned about me as an individual. It didn't have anything to do with basketball or being an athlete. It was about me as a human being.

Still, I felt as though I had earned it. When I started at Nordstrom, I'd decided that if I had to be a bus boy I'd be the best damn bus boy, the best dishwasher in the world. I wasn't going to let anything anybody said, anything they thought, keep me from reaching my goals. I worked that job for months without taking a day off. If something was spilled on the floor, I was the first one there with a mop, cleaning it up. If crumbs or ketchup or food was spilled on a table, I'd be there first with a rag to wipe it up. I moved from busboy to dishwasher to sandwich maker to working the cash register. I'd worked my tail off, and it felt good to have someone notice and appreciate it.

They had offered me a chance, and although I was a little afraid of tackling my speech problem, I decided that if that's what it would take to get ahead, I'd deal with it.

14

MOVING UP

I never played the victim.

OW, IT SO HAPPENED THAT WHEN I took the bus to work each morning, I passed a place called the Seattle Speech & Hearing Clinic, which I believe was funded by the United Way. Since it was near my job, it seemed like the perfect spot. And when I told the Nordstrom executives about it, they had a representative call and set up an appointment for an evaluation. I went in for my interview in February of 1986, and I talked to Susan Hamilton, a young lady who had just arrived in Seattle. She didn't really know much about basketball or who I was, but we hit it off immediately. She accepted me as a client, and in May I began therapy.

First Steps in Speech Therapy

For the next two months, I went through a very intense program. She had me coming in four times a week for two hours each day. From the very first day, I was excited and enthusiastic. I had been disappointed with the speech therapists I'd seen during my playing days, because all they did was have me read. During the evaluation session, Susan had indicated that she would take a much different approach. And when I arrived, I was ready and anxious to get started. I think that I may have even surprised her a little when I told her what my goal was.

"I want to be a great speaker," I said. "I want to be so good that I can stand up before thousands of people and deliver a speech."

She just smiled. I don't think she really knew how determined I was at that point.

We started from scratch, working in what she called the therapy room. At first, I worked on saying simple, two-syllable words clearly, without stuttering. I'd concentrate on getting out one word at a time, slowly pronouncing it, then pausing, then moving on to another word. We stretched that to two words, then three, and so on. But it was much more than rote recitation—we also worked on eye contact, breathing, phrasing, and, because she had pointed out that I tensed up and pushed too hard on consonant sounds, she tried to get me to emphasize the vowel sounds.

I was working hard at it, and almost immediately I began to see some significant advancement. After the first week, I reached a point where I could even string whole sentences together without stumbling or tripping myself up, if I concentrated on what I'd learned and spoke slowly. I was never late, and I didn't miss a single session with Susan. I put everything I had into it, and my dedication paid off. After only sixteen sessions, Susan told me that I had gotten through the first step—I'd achieved fluency in the therapy room.

Now, when I first heard that, I was thrilled. I thought I'd gotten over the hump. That's when Susan warned me that I had a long way to go. For the next month, I continued seeing her four times each week, but the emphasis changed. We moved on to the "transfer stage," and I began trying to apply some of the techniques I'd learned during the first month to everyday situations in my life.

I carried a tape recorder with me, and throughout the day, when I talked to people I'd ask if it was all right to record the conversation. It was a little embarrassing for me, but most people didn't mind, and I was determined to push forward. I started by recording talks with friends and family; that was the easiest because that's when I was most relaxed. Then I began taping conversations with people I didn't know—my daughter's hairdresser or strangers I met at the bus stop or in the bar where I stopped for a beer. Finally, I moved on to some of the supervisors and higher-ups at Nordstrom. That was the toughest assignment for me. I'd always been a little uptight around authority figures like teachers and my immediate superiors at jobs, but both Susan and I were surprised at how well I did on those tapes.

Back at the clinic, Susan would go over the tapes with me. We talked about each one, and she pointed out differences she saw in the way I spoke to various people. Soon I began to see that the way I felt and thought about the people I talked to affected my speech much more than I realized. And as I understood it more, I began to gain some control over it. In a way, it was like practicing basketball. You had to drill in the fundamentals, get them down pat, and then analyze the actual game situation and figure out how to deal with specific encounters, how to use the fundamentals under pressure. By the end of my second month of therapy I had improved even more. I was gradually getting better and better.

So Much for Moonlighting

Meanwhile, the first of a few problems that I'd have at Nordstrom reared up. My disability payments and welfare support had been cut off when I started working. And after my first few months on the job, I realized that I wasn't earning enough money to make ends meet. There was no way I could support myself and make child support payments to my ex-wife and kids on my salary alone. I needed a second job to survive, so I took a part-time job as a bus driver for the Metro Bus Company.

I worked there for over six months, and during that time I had a very hectic schedule. After leaving Nordstrom in the afternoon, I had to catch a bus and ride out to the Metro bus terminal, which was about eight miles from downtown Seattle. I'd rush into the depot, change into my driver's uniform, and hustle onto the bus. I drove back into downtown Seattle and made my evening rounds before returning the bus to the terminal and getting a ride back into the city.

I wasn't aware of it, but Nordstrom had an unwritten rule forbidding employees to work a second job. And after I began the therapy sessions with Susan at the clinic, Jim Dickinson, one of my supervisors, found out that I was moonlighting. There was a big to-do about it, and Dickinson pushed for his bosses to fire me. Finally, I gave up my bus driving career, so Nordstrom didn't let me go. Still, that incident put a damper on the friendship I thought I had with my supervisor.

My First Promotion

At the time, I was still stumbling over words when I was too excited or nervous, but the difference between my speech when I started therapy and the way I spoke four months later was like night and day. Susan had reduced our sessions from four to two times a week, and we were still working on transferring the techniques I'd learned to real-life encounters. I was amazed at the progress I'd made, and I think she was also. And with every advance I saw, I took heart and worked even harder. I had made some dramatic improvements, and it was about that time that Susan told me what one of the owners at Nordstrom had said.

"There were times when Bob was like a scared butterfly," he had told her, "but now when he comes up to the table to talk to us he looks us directly in the eye and says exactly what's on his mind. The progress is amazing."

Shortly after she told me that, I received my first promotion. I was moved from the downtown store and restaurant to the catering department, which was in Ballard, a small community just outside Seattle. My job was to help the caterers set up and prepare for parties and large corporate affairs. We catered parties with hundreds of guests, and some of them went on until the next morning. The menus included nearly every kind of food you could imagine—from simple things like finger sandwiches, quiche, and crudités to fancy stuff like crab claws, caviar, pâté de foie gras, and the finest of wines.

I usually worked in the warehouse or commissary, where the serving utensils and dishes, drinks, and some of the staple foods were stored. My new boss was Art Nelson. I'd seen him around the commissary before, but I'd never had to work with him directly. He was a little guy, only about 5 feet 6 inches, but, as I quickly discovered, he was a big problem for me.

I Got to Stay Here

Although I was excited about the promotion and threw myself into the new job, Art was on my case every day when I came to work. I was speaking much better, but I was still nervous around my immediate bosses, and a lot of times I'd fall back into old habits when I talked to Art. He teased me about my speech and kidded me about the way black athletes talked. "Hey, Bob," he'd say, "did you see that interview with that football player on ESPN last night?"

I'd always say no, I didn't see it, but that didn't stop him.

"Every other word that boy said was, 'Ya' know . . . ya' know.' Hell, if I knew, I wouldn't have been listening to that dummy," he'd laugh.

Art never let up, and it wasn't easy. But I tried to ignore his cracks about black athletes and concentrate on my work.

He kept the pressure on me, and whenever I made the slightest mistake, he'd jump down my throat. I was convinced that he was trying to force me to quit. For instance, the Ballard warehouse was a huge building, seemed like it was a mile long; and although I later found out that it had been mopped only once a week before I started, Art had me mopping it three times each week.

Part of my job was delivering doughnuts, rolls, and other pastries, baked goods, and staples to Nordstrom outlets around the city. I went into the commissary at about five o'clock in the morning, picked up the items requested by the various cafes, and delivered them before opening time. Besides the baked goods, my list included things like milk, butter, and other basic ingredients. One morning, as I unloaded an order from the truck, I discovered that I had forgotten to bring along the brown sugar requested by a cafe manager. I was aware of my mistake, but I didn't think it was a big thing. I just told the manager that I was sorry, and said I'd go back to the warehouse and get it.

I'm not sure what set him off that morning—maybe something had gone wrong at home—but the cafe manager blew up when he heard that I had to come back with the sugar. Before I left, he called Art. When I got back to the warehouse, Art and his assistant, a German woman named Sue Diamond who had been hostile to me from the day I started, were waiting at the door. Art got in my face immediately.

"Can you read?" he shouted, pushing a requisition slip in front of my face.

"Sure I can."

"Well, what does this say?"

"Brr . . . brown—shhh . . . sugar," I said. I was nervous and the stuttering flared up.

He stared at me for a moment, then he looked over at Sue with an odd grin on his face. Suddenly, he turned back toward me and hauled off and kicked me. I couldn't believe it. Kicked me hard, right in the back of my calf. It was almost as if he were daring me to react. And it took all of my willpower to keep from tearing into him. I was peering down at him, biting my tongue to keep from going off, and he was looking at me with this strange grin on his face—like he was thinking, *Go on, swing at me.*

Then he stepped back and said, "Don't ever forget the damn brown sugar again," and walked away.

162   I'm not sure how I managed to control myself, but I just looked at him and shook my head. I didn't let him know it, but my leg was throbbing with pain and I was mad as hell. I felt like grabbing that little redneck and wringing his throat right there. At the same time, I knew he was goading me. My job was at

stake. Hell, despite Art, my speech was improving and things were looking up. I said to myself: *I can't hit this guy. Shit, I got to stay here. I got to stay.*

When I told a few friends about that incident later on, they said, "Damn, man, if it had been me, I would've kicked his ass." I'd have done this and I'd have done that. But I knew that if I had retaliated, all he had to do was say I hit him first. I was the only black person in that division and I would have been gone. So I let it pass—just walked away.

Friends in High Places

Despite the run-ins with Art, I was working hard and doing well. One advantage I had at work was that I got along well with the owners of the store. It was odd, but while I often froze up and stuttered terribly around my direct supervisors, I was pretty relaxed with the owners. Unlike most of the other employees, I was never in awe of them. Most of the middle-management people like Art Nelson and Jim Dickinson were timid and deferential when they were around Bruce and John Nordstrom or other executives. They might pass a few comments, small talk like, "How are the family and kids . . . Good weekend—play any golf?" Then they would hurry off and get back to their jobs.

But I had a great rapport with the owners and executives; they were patient with me, so I was usually relaxed and didn't stutter too badly. Even when I began and was doing truly menial jobs, they would stop by and strike up conversations with me. A lot of the time, of course, they wanted to talk about sports and NBA basketball. Most guys realize how hard it is to make it in professional sports. And nobody understands that better than the guys who have climbed to the top and become successful in the corporate world. They had to fight just as hard as athletes to make it in a world that's equally cutthroat and difficult to excel in. They have a lot of respect for athletes, and since they're secure about their own positions, they're not afraid to show it. I think that's part of the reason you see guys like Donald Trump hanging out with athletes like Mike Tyson.

I respected the top guys at Nordstrom, but because I'd tasted success and been at the top of my own field, I wasn't intimidated. I never tried to butter them up or ingratiate myself. Yeah, I wanted to move up and be as successful as they were in that world, but they were just people to me. And that's how I treated them.

I think that's why we got along as well as we did. We spent a lot of time talking about basketball, but our conversations weren't limited to just sports. We chatted about politics, and they'd ask about my ideas on improving things on the job. They'd talk about their personal lives and tell me what they thought about this employee or that one. Somehow, they knew I wouldn't reveal what they'd said. I enjoyed those conversations, and I was usually very relaxed around those guys.

Of course, I suspected that if I had been completely unknown, just your average employee, it would never have happened. I would still have been stammering and stuttering there in the kitchen—that is, if I had gotten a job at all. But for whatever reason, they sensed something different about my attitude. I never took on that inferior approach that a lot of employees adopted. Even though I was embarrassed about what I was doing on the job, deep down I felt as though I was equal to anyone I met. I never played the victim. I think that's what allowed me to get on so well with the owners and executives, and that definitely helped me move up at Nordstrom.

Still, my rapport with the store's executives wasn't always beneficial. Soon after my first promotion, I discovered that it was a double-edged sword. I guess a lot of employees felt that I was getting preferential treatment, and there were problems with some of the middle-management people when I started moving up. It may have just been jealousy or sour grapes, but during the first few years at the store it seemed like a few people were trying to cut me off at every corner. It began with the complaints about my moonlighting as a bus driver, and later one of my supervisors accused me of theft because of an eight-dollar discrepancy on an expense receipt. Someone even started a rumor that I was a pimp and had three girls working on the streets. The accusations were false, of course, and nothing came of them. But still, there was something about my independence and confidence that irritated some people. John and Bruce Nordstrom and most of the other executives were always supportive and encouraging, but I faced a lot of resistance from people below them. And nobody was more of a thorn in my side than Art Nelson.

Promotion and Vindication

At the end of 1986, about four months after the confrontation with Art and Sue over forgetting the brown sugar, I was promoted again. I began working with a team of people who traveled outside Seattle to assist in catering company affairs. From 1985 through 1989, Nordstrom expanded rapidly; they were opening new stores all the way down the coast to San Francisco and the Bay area. My job was to help set up those grand-opening celebrations. They always had the best of food and wine for those affairs, and often there were five thousand or more guests. I had to make sure that everything was set up correctly, then, when the party was over, assist in the cleanup and disposal or repackaging of leftovers, glasses, trays, and whatnot. They had to be loaded into these large, forty-foot trucks, returned to the warehouse, and unloaded. Usually there was help, but occasionally I was left to do this by myself.

Art Nelson was still my boss, and it seemed that he tried to hassle me or make the job harder every chance he got. One night when we were in San Francisco, he called at about midnight and said that he wanted a truck unloaded by one o'clock the next afternoon. He wanted me to unload it, sweep it out, then wash and stack all the glasses and trays. I think he knew that, starting that late at night, there would be no one to help me.

The warehouse was in this rough section of the city, and since it was so dark, deserted, and desolate, I spent a lot of time looking over my shoulder. It was scary as hell, and it took most of the night to unload that truck. But I did it, and by seven o'clock I had finished. Then I had to start washing the trays and glasses. I was tired but I kept at it, and about ten that morning, they sent some Mexican workers out to help me. Art showed up a few hours after they arrived.

When the help arrived, we finished washing the glasses and trays. Afterward we dried them, put them in plastic bags, and stacked them. But because we were rushing to finish by one o'clock, a few trays were left slightly damp. Art watched as we finished the job. He checked everything we did, including the trays, but he didn't say anything about the damp ones. At about twelve-thirty, he smiled and said, "Bob, you can go home now—you can go back to Seattle."

"All right," I said, "I'm tired."

I went back to Seattle, and the next morning I was awakened by a call from the catering manager, R. J. Selfridge. He had hardly said hello before he told me that I was fired.

I was shocked. "Why?" I asked, "What did I do?"

He told me Art had said that I was incompetent—that I'd left a lot of trays wet and he was fed up with my sloppy work. He never wanted to work with me again. I tried to explain that I'd unloaded that eighteen-wheeler by myself, then washed and dried and stacked thousands of trays and glasses. By then, I'd slipped back into some old speech habits and started stuttering and stammering. I was pissed off, frustrated, and afraid that I'd lost my job. "You telling me that after all that," I finally blurted out, "you're firing me for leaving a few trays wet?"

He didn't answer—just hung up on me.

166

I tried calling Jim Dickinson, the restaurant manager, but he wouldn't even answer my call. So I went downtown to see him. His secretary said he wasn't in, but the door to his office was cracked and I saw him inside. I said, "All right, all right. I'll just sit here until he comes back." I stayed there all day, but he left by another exit and didn't return.

The next day, I went to see John Nordstrom and his brother Bruce. I was so nervous I could barely get the story out, but I told them what had happened. Finally, Bruce said, "Look, you've been a good worker for us, Bob. Let me try and find out what really happened."

They called around the stores and talked to people I had worked with, talked to the caterers and cafe manager; everyone said I was a dedicated hard worker. They also found that I hadn't given anybody any trouble, and with the exception of Art, no one had any real complaints about my work. A few days later, they called me back into the office and said, "Bob, we can't find anything wrong with your work. Everybody seems to think you're doing a fine job."

They told me they'd try to work something out but that returning to my old job with Art would pose a problem. Then Bruce asked me what Art had been doing while I was unloading the truck in San Francisco. "Well," I said, "I don't really know. But he wasn't there."

His face turned red as fire. He just said, "OK, I'll see what I can do about your job," and thanked me. About a week later, Bruce called and said, "It's all right, Bob, you got your job back. You can report to work tomorrow."

They brought me back and no further questions were asked. I was still working in the catering department at the warehouse, but I had a different boss. Then, about six weeks later, Art was fired. I never found out exactly why they let him go—but on his last day, after he had packed his stuff and was walking out the door, I hollered out to him.

"Hey, Art! Ya . . . ya . . . you know. Ya' know," I said. He looked kind of confused at first. Then I said, "Thought maybe even you would *know something* by now, my man!" He stomped out of the commissary, and I never saw him again.

167

15

AN EFFECTIVE COMMUNICATOR

*I realized I had a real gift for storytelling, for
using the ups and downs, the successes and
mistakes of my life to inspire other people.*

I N MAY OF 1987, I MADE MY first public speech. My therapy sessions had been decreased to once a week, and I was still taping conversations and working on transference. But I was
anxious to face the real test, to stand up and address a live audience. I worked on that speech for weeks with Susan, and finally
I found myself standing on stage at the Langston Hughes Center in Seattle delivering a talk to about three hundred young
people who had just received their general equivalency diplomas.

Everybody was surprised with the way it went over. In fact,
I think I may have even surprised myself. I'd been a little nervous beforehand, but the moment I got behind the podium and
began speaking, I was as confident as could be—it was game
time. For me, it was the beginning of a fantasy come true. I
wasn't speaking before the sea of people that I'd always imagined. But when I told my story that first night, when I saw how
those kids honestly reacted and related to the struggle, the highs
and lows I'd gone through, even I was moved. I think that's why
the speech went as well as it did. I was being myself up there,
and I think those young people in the audience saw that and
respected it.

Susan was there also. And later she told me that although she
knew I'd made great strides in speech technique, in pronouncing words, and in properly developing fluency, she was truly
impressed with my ability to capture the audience's attention

and hold it. Her comments meant as much to me as the applause I received after that speech. The dream was still a long way from being fulfilled, but I left that center knowing that, if I worked even harder, I could make it a reality.

I Could Be a Great Motivational Speaker

During the next few months, I kept at it, giving a few little speeches around Seattle whenever I got the chance. Mind you, although I was grateful for the opportunities that Nordstrom had given me, I wasn't entirely satisfied with my job at the company. I still longed to get back into basketball, and it was during that time that I approached Dick Motta and a few others about a coaching position. Nothing came of it. I was disappointed, but I directed my energies to working at the commissary and began working even harder to improve my speech.

By then, some reporters in Seattle had heard about the speeches, and I began getting some attention in the local press. My bosses at Nordstrom were also aware of the talks. They called Susan to congratulate her on her work and tell her how pleased they were with my progress. Then in July, Nordstrom arranged for me to give a speech at a high school banquet in Rockford, Illinois, just outside of Chicago. Several thousand people were expected to attend.

It was a great opportunity for me. I knew that many company officials would be there, and it would be the first time that I spoke before such a large group. Susan and I worked on the speech for weeks, changing this and that, adding material about Nordstrom and the opportunity that they'd given me. We made sure that I was well prepared. When we flew out to Chicago, I was excited about the challenge, but surprisingly I wasn't nervous or tense.

As it turned out, I gave one of the best speeches that I'd given until that time. At the end, I got a standing ovation. Susan and the Nordstrom executives were out in the audience beaming. I think that's when I first realized I had a real gift for storytelling, for using the ups and downs, the successes and mistakes of my life to inspire other people. Afterward, Susan told me that she thought I could be a great motivational speaker.

A Giant Step Forward

A few months later, I was promoted to corporate director of health and sanitation for Nordstrom's restaurant division. It was a giant step forward. Not only did my salary increase to a point where I was able to finally afford to take better care of my kids, but the job also required that I be on the road, working alone much of the time. And since I'd always enjoyed traveling and being on my own, it was a welcome change from both the closely supervised work I'd been doing before and the office politics that came with it.

Basically, I was working as a health inspector. My job was to check out all of Nordstrom's restaurants and cafes, making sure that the food was being kept and served correctly. The company had its own standards, which were pretty high, and of course I had to see that there were no city health code violations. That job took me to all the stores along the West Coast, including San Francisco, Los Angeles, and San Diego, as well as to the new stores, which at that time were opening as far east as New Jersey.

A New Son

By 1988, things were looking up at my job and in therapy, and I was steadily improving as a speaker. But it was an entirely different story on the home front. My personal life was becoming even more unsettled and chaotic.

My relationship with Natalie had hit the skids near the end of the previous year after she discovered that she was pregnant. When she told me about it, I asked her to marry me. But she refused. She didn't want any part of marriage, at least not with me, and for some reason she seemed angry that she was having a child. Then one day during the winter of 1987, she just exploded. She said she wanted me out of the house that very day. I tried to convince her to let me stay because I wanted to be there when my child was born. But nothing I said changed her mind. She refused to budge.

I packed up my clothes and personal belongings and arranged to move back to Kirkland, where I stayed at the home of my friend Mike Clanton. It was a good-size house with a large back-yard, and I had my own room and all the privacy I needed.

Then on Mother's Day in May 1988, my seventh child was born. It was a boy, Nathaniel, and although Natalie and I weren't getting along and didn't live together, I was very proud of that child. I tried to see him whenever I could, but because of the tension between his mother and me, the visits were kept to a minimum. When I was there, Natalie hovered around like I was a stranger, and you could almost feel the chill in the room. Still, I loved Nathaniel, and if I could have been there more often, I would have gladly spent more time with him.

After the split with Natalie, there was really no one special in my life. I went out some, dated occasionally, and socialized with the guys at the Appointment and a few other places around Seattle. But most of my energy and time were spent at work. My latest promotion at Nordstrom had given me a great opportunity, a chance to prove myself, and I wanted to take advantage of it. The owners of the company, Jim, Bruce, and John Nordstrom, were among the finest people I'd met. They seemed to care about their employees, and they had taken a chance on me. I didn't want to let them down, so I put every-thing I had into my job and improving as a speaker.

Surrendering Dreams of Eloquence

By the summer of 1988, I was convinced that I had gotten as much as I could from speech therapy. I called Susan and told her

I felt that I was ready to stop. She warned me that there was really no cure for stuttering. "Regression or relapse is part of the process," she said. "The best you can hope to do is keep it under control."

I really respected her opinion, but I was determined. So one day I went to her and said, "Look, Susan, I think I'm ready to quit. I got this thing beat, I'm never going to stutter again."

Over the long haul, of course, she was right. My problem with stuttering didn't just go away. I'd slip back a little, fall into some of the bad habits that had bedeviled me at the start. So although I stopped seeing her for formal training sessions, she continued working with me during the next few years. The company was arranging more and more speeches for me, and Susan was still helping me prepare those talks and giving me tips on little things that I was doing wrong. She had left the clinic to take a teaching job at Seattle Pacific University, and I went to see her nearly every time I had to speak.

During that time, I saw that I'd been way too optimistic about never stuttering again. Susan and I talked about it a lot, and I finally realized that it was a battle I'd have to fight for the rest of my life. Still, I was steadily improving. I'd learned not to tense up or let it bother me when I tripped over a few words. And as Susan pointed out, sometimes those glitches made my talks more effective. They allowed the audience to identify with me, and when I talked about the times when I couldn't get a single word out without stammering and pausing, a slight hitch in my speech reminded listeners of how far I had come.

I was never happy with those slips, and I still dreamed of being the smoothest, most eloquent orator in the world. But I also began to understand and accept something that Susan emphasized over and over. "The real goal," she always told me, "is to become an effective communicator." After a while, I truly felt that with her help I'd reached that level. Although later on, after she opened a private practice and began teaching at the University of Washington, we didn't see each other as often, I've never forgotten how important she was in guiding me through the most difficult challenge of my life.

Another Promotion

I continued working as a sanitation inspector for Nordstrom's restaurants until early in 1990, but more and more I was being asked to appear before civic groups or at various corporate functions and tell the story of my life and my struggle to move up in the company. Then later that year, I received another promotion. I was given a job as director of human resources, which meant that I was directly involved in enlisting minority employees. I was in charge of recruiting them, then helping to set up training and management programs.

It also required that I travel and speak even more frequently. The job took me all over the country, where I visited and spoke at high schools, colleges, culinary schools, restaurants, and business or civic conferences. Using my own story as an example, I talked about Nordstrom's continued expansion and pitched the equal opportunity policy that was one of the company's chief concerns. It was a great job for me. I felt good about making a contribution to the community by trying to guide young people to a company that promised to give them a real chance, and at the same time I was improving as a speaker.

It was in 1990 that I really began to feel that I'd turned my life around. Financially I was doing well, and for the first time I really felt that I'd turned my disability into something positive. I began to believe that I could support myself by speaking. In the back of my mind, I still had a desire to somehow get back into basketball on some level. But Nordstrom had treated me well and given me every chance to prove myself, and I was happy there. I had no intention of going out to look for another job.

That fall, I left Kirkland and rented an apartment in downtown Seattle. I also called Betty and told her that I was finally able to get a house for her and our kids. Near the end of the year, I bought them a house in Kirkland.

Then about three months later, just as I began to think things were settling down, I got a call from Betty. She told me that caring for the children was too much of a burden, and she needed some time for herself. A couple of weeks later, she found an apartment in Bothell and took our youngest child, Kerry, with her. I moved into the Kirkland house with my five older kids.

Although Betty was determined to try to do something for herself after six years of devoting her life to the children, she didn't just disappear. She helped out at crunch times and never made the kids feel that they had been deserted. Still, it was tough being thrust back into the role of an on-the-scene, every-day parent, particularly since my job kept me on the road for much of the time. On the other hand, I had seen my kids only infrequently since my divorce from Betty, and I tried to take advantage of the opportunity to really get to know them again. We spent over a year together in Kirkland, and during that time I gained custody of Keith, Barri, and Kerry, who were still under the age of 18. Despite my absences and travel, I think I reestablished a bond with the kids that has lasted until the present.

And Another Promotion

Meanwhile, my career at Nordstrom was picking up steam. The speeches that I'd been giving as human resources director were attracting attention at Nordstrom and in the media. In telling the story of starting at the bottom, struggling to overcome my speech problem with the aid and support of company executives, and rising to the corporate level at Nordstrom, I was becoming a much more effective speaker and increasing my value to the company. But I was also helping to improve the Nordstrom image, particularly with regard to its employee relationships. During that period, I traveled with the owners a few times and spoke at corporate meetings and civil rights conferences. Many times I was the only black person at those meetings. And late in the fall of 1991, after I had given a talk before some corporate bigwigs, John Nordstrom asked if I'd be willing to move from human resources and become the company's spokesperson.

A week or so later, I was promoted to corporate spokesperson for the Nordstrom company. Now, in reality I was doing much the same thing I'd been doing before. The main differences were that I was no longer responsible for setting up minority programs and that my speeches were not focused solely on Nordstrom's relationship to its minority employees. Instead, I tried to relate my story to the company's progressive attitude toward all its employees. I still spoke at high schools, universities, and colleges, but more and more I talked to business organizations and civic or rights groups like the Rotary Club or the NAACP. It was a challenge, and I enjoyed every minute of it. By early 1992 I had settled into the job, and I felt that I'd nearly reached my goal. I was finally being recognized solely for my speaking ability. I had become the effective communicator that my therapist and I had talked about, and except for my own personal satisfaction, nothing pleased me more than knowing that Susan Hamilton was just as proud as I was.

Later that summer, I received a call from Bobby Wilson, a former Chicago Bulls teammate. He was working for the Little City Foundation, an organization that raised money for the support and care of children and adults with disabilities in the Chicago area. His job was to contact former Bulls players to appear along with some of the current players at a series of fund-raising events. The team had changed ownership since the days when Bobby and I played, and Bobby assured me that the new owners would welcome me. When he asked if I'd come to town for a luncheon, I agreed right away. It was a cause that I could easily identify with. I filled him in on what I was doing, and almost as an afterthought, I said that I'd be glad to speak if he thought it would help. Bobby thought it was a great idea, and a couple of weeks later I flew into Chicago for the luncheon at the Hyatt Regency Hotel.

176

Maybe it was the foundation's work with people with disabilities that inspired me; I'm not sure. But I gave one of the most moving speeches of my life that afternoon. It was one of a series of luncheons set up to convince potential contributors to participate in Little City's annual fund-raising dinner, so the audience included ballplayers, a large group of corporate executives, and representatives from the Bulls public relations department. Very few people in Chicago knew much about what I'd done after I left basketball, and I think they were all amazed when I told the story of what had happened to me and how, with Nordstrom's help, I'd overcome my disability. When I finished, nearly everybody in that room was crying, including Bobby and me. They gave me a standing ovation that must have lasted for four or five minutes. And the next day, the press was all over the story. I was thrilled at the response, and I did a few interviews with reporters from the newspapers and local radio and television stations before leaving. But when I flew back to Seattle, I had no idea that the speech would have such a great impact on my life.

Chicago Beckons

Being in Chicago, meeting with and speaking before some of my former teammates, had set off an old yearning to somehow get back into basketball. And although I had no complaints about my job at Nordstrom, I couldn't help daydreaming about it for the next few days.

Then a week after I returned home, two things happened to whet my appetite even more. First, the Little City Foundation's directors called and asked if I would like to speak at their fundraising dinner in September. I knew that the Bulls and many of their players were involved, and I saw it as another chance to briefly touch base with a game that I still loved even though I had left it. I immediately said yes to that.

Then a few days later, I received a call from the Bulls office inviting me to be their guest during the championship play-off series against the Portland Trail Blazers. After the final game, when they won the title, Jerry Reinsdorf (the team CEO), Steve Schanwald (the team's VP of marketing and broadcast), and Jerry Krause (the VP of basketball operations), asked me to attend the postgame party. Steve Kerr, Bill Cartwright, and

177

many other players were there along with their wives or girl-friends and the entire Bulls organization, including the owners and executives. It was their second straight championship, and the celebration was intense. I had been back to a few old-timers games in the past, but I really began to respect the new owners that night. They treated me as if I was part of the team, one of the guys who had helped them win. I talked to Jerry Reinsdorf that evening, and he said he'd heard about my speech and how impressed everyone was with it. There wasn't much of a chance to talk in all that confusion, but he said he'd keep in touch. All in all, I had a great time, but I still returned to Seattle feeling a little sad about being separated from the basketball world. I was returning to a great job in Seattle, but I was still daydreaming.

The very next week, I received another call from the Chicago Bulls. It was a conference call from Steve Schanwald and Jerry Reinsdorf. They told me that they had heard about my speech at the fund-raising luncheon and had been impressed when I visited during the championship play-offs. Then they said that if I was available, they wanted me to come back to Chicago and join the team as director of community relations.

When I heard that, I was so excited I almost dropped the phone. But after I collected myself, I didn't give them an immediate response. I didn't say yes. I didn't say no. I wanted to at least think about it overnight.

That evening I sat down by myself and weighed my choices. The Bulls were offering me a great job with more money and an opportunity to return to the sports world that I loved. Still, I felt a tremendous allegiance to the Nordstrom company. They had helped me pull myself up and get my life together. I was indebted to them. But I also knew that things were changing at Nordstrom. John, Bruce, and Jim Nordstrom were getting up in age, and a younger generation of executives was taking over. They had a different philosophy, and I had the feeling that things might be changing radically soon. They were set to diversify the company, and a lot of people had already started losing their jobs. Others were being moved and shifted around to new positions. I thought about the situation all evening, and finally made up my mind. Chicago was the best place for me; in my heart I knew it. That night I got down on my knees and thanked the Lord for keeping me strong along the way. I also prayed that I was making the right decision.

The next day, I called the Bulls and told them that I accepted their offer. Later I went in to John Nordstrom's office and told him that I'd been offered a job with the Chicago Bulls and had decided to take it. He asked if I was sure I was doing the right thing for myself, and I told him that I'd thought about it and felt that it was time to move on. I thanked him for everything that Nordstrom had done for me and tried to smile. I was excited about going back to Chicago, but I really respected the Nordstrom owners. I couldn't help feeling a little sad.

When I had told my younger kids that I was going back to work for the Bulls, they were really excited about returning to Chicago with me. Then at the last minute, Keith decided to stay with his mother. He was playing on a pretty good high school basketball team in Seattle, and he thought they had a chance at winning the state championship the following year. But Barri, my youngest daughter, and Kerry, my youngest son, were anxious to leave, and in August we boarded a train in downtown Seattle and started the cross-country trip.

I had mixed feelings as the train pulled away. I was excited about returning to the Bulls, but I didn't really know what to expect. It took two and a half days to get to Chicago, and I remember pacing nervously up and down the train during much of that trip. Sometimes I'd go to the lounge car and just sit by the window, looking up at the mountains or staring off into space. I thought about the incredible string of events that had led to my return. I'd worked hard to drag myself up from the bottom, from nowhere. But I'd also had a lot of help, and I'd been lucky. I knew that, and a few times each day, even when I was with Barri and Kerry, I closed my eyes and thanked the Lord for delivering me.

I also thought about my old friends and the good times I'd had in Chicago. There had been newspaper stories about my returning to the Bulls, and I knew that many of my friends had read them. I was anxious to get back to see them. So although I was a little tense, it was an exciting, memorable trip. And by the time we arrived at Union Station, I was ready to get started at the new job. It wouldn't be quite like playing for the Bulls, but at least I was part of the team again—part of the game.

16

SWEET HOME CHICAGO

*It seemed like I was on a roll
that wouldn't stop.*

WHEN WE ARRIVED IN CHICAGO, it took a couple of weeks for me and the kids to settle into our apartment in Buffalo Grove, a suburb northwest of Chicago. They got set up at their new school, and I began orientation with the Bulls public relations section right away. Within a few weeks, I'd started as director of community relations.

The job didn't require a lot of adjustments for me since it was much like what I'd been doing as the corporate spokesperson at Nordstrom. Basically, I became the Chicago Bulls spokesperson, a kind of goodwill ambassador, representing the team at various functions related to their image in the community. At the start, I worked with the educational program, appearing at local schools and talking to kids about sports and education. I'd tell the story of my rise in the NBA, the crash after I left the league, and the struggle to overcome personal problems and start a new life. I urged kids to stay in school and get an education and, most important, to never make the mistake of giving up and looking at themselves as victims.

I'd always loved talking to kids, and the Bulls were deeply involved with educational programs in Chicago, so it was a perfect way for me to start out. The team had given me a new sport utility vehicle as part of my contract, and I traveled over two hundred miles a day visiting schools all over the city and in the suburbs and surrounding areas. I spoke a dozen or more times a week, and soon I was appearing at meetings of civic organizations, fund-raisers for battered women's shelters or the Little League, golf tournaments, parades, and other charity events. I also spoke at employee rallies held by Budweiser, Gatorade, the Miller Brewery, and other companies that were corporate sponsors of the team.

Things were rolling along just fine that first year. My kids were happy, I was doing well on the job, and my social life had picked up. I dated a little during the first few months after I returned to Chicago, but I spent most of my spare time getting reacquainted with old friends and hanging out with the guys. My old buddies were happy to see me back on the scene, and I was just as glad to see them. There were a few bars and restaurants around town where most of them hung out, and when I wasn't working or spending time with the kids, that's usually where you'd find me.

One of the most popular spots was the President's Lounge on 75th Street. All the former athletes stopped in to have a drink and swap stories about their playing days or talk about the young players and current teams. If you wanted to meet anybody who had done anything in sports in the Chicago area, that was the place to be. I loved going in there and reminiscing with the old gang, so I'd stop in once or twice a week. Even so, after a while I realized that there was something missing. I knew I had to find someone special, someone with whom I could share my new life.

Then about six months after returning, I finally met a woman I really liked. Her name was Rachel Dixson, and I met her while speaking at a teachers conference at the Sheraton Hotel in downtown Chicago. I spotted her with a group of teachers before I went up to the stage to speak, and right off the bat she caught my eye. She had this big smile, bubbly personality, and gorgeous Georgia-peach complexion. I was interested, but I didn't have a chance to say anything. Then, as I was leaving, she ran up and started a conversation. That's when I found out that she was a southern girl who had grown up in Pickens, Mississippi, and graduated from Alcorn State in nearby Lorman. She had taught in the Chicago school system for thirteen years, and when I talked to her I discovered that she was even smarter and wittier than she was attractive. Before I left, I got her phone number, and a few days later I called and asked her to have dinner with me.

We hit it off from the start, and during the next few weeks we went out several times. I even visited her school and met her class. The thing that got my attention at her job was the way she got along with the kids. They really loved her, and you could see that she enjoyed being around them. The relationship took off quickly, and about six weeks after we met I took her with me on a trip to Cincinnati, where she met my brother Errol. We had a terrific time out there, and when we returned I knew that she was the woman of my dreams. I was madly in love.

Then, a few months later, I decided to move out of my Buffalo Grove apartment. While I was searching for a new place, Barri, Kerry, and I moved into Rachel's home on Artesian Boulevard in Chicago. We got to know each other even better during that time, and it seemed that my children liked her nearly as much as I did. I found a new apartment in Naperville, another Chicago suburb, later that year, and my relationship with Rachel continued growing.

Encouraging My Kids to Stay in School

Everything was looking up for me at that time. It seemed like I was on a roll that wouldn't stop. In fact, the only serious problem I had during that time was with my kids. During the summer of 1993, after he graduated from high school in Seattle, my son Keith came to Chicago to stay with me, Barri, and Kerry. Then one evening when I returned from a speaking engagement, I discovered that my ex-wife Betty had come to Chicago and taken Barri and Kerry back to Seattle with her.

When I found out what had happened, I was disappointed and hurt. I guess the thing that disturbed me most was that nobody told me they were going. But I was also worried about their education. Both of the kids were doing well in school. In

fact, as a junior Barri had a great year on her high school basketball team. Scouts had come around, and she was on the verge
of being offered a basketball scholarship at the University of
Illinois. But during her senior year back in Seattle, she didn't get
much playing time because the coach had already decided on his
starting lineup. She was heartbroken, and after the basketball
season ended, she returned to Chicago and graduated from her
old school in Buffalo Grove. Kerry, who was in junior high
school, stayed in Seattle with his mother and recently graduated
from high school.

I worked hard to make sure that my younger kids had the
opportunity to go to college during those years, but the battle
didn't turn out the way I'd hoped. I convinced Keith to enroll
at my old alma mater, Southern University, for the fall semester in 1993. And after Barri graduated in 1994, I also sent her
to Southern. But neither one of them liked Baton Rouge or the
South. They had grown up in a fairly large northern city, and
they hated the heat and the down-home, small-town college
atmosphere. Every time I talked to them they complained about
the school and let me know that they wanted to leave. I encouraged them to stick it out and do the best that they could. But
nothing I said about the value of a college education got
through to them—they didn't want to hear it.

Keith dropped out of school during the second term. I was
disappointed when I heard what he'd done, and the following
summer I went out to Seattle to try to convince him to give it
another try. It took some effort, but when he found out that his
sister Barri would be enrolling, he finally agreed to return to
Southern. I felt great after he made his decision, and when I
returned to Chicago, I really thought that both of them would
go on to complete their education at Southern. It didn't turn out
that way.

Keith fell in love with a young girl who lived back home in
Seattle and dropped out of school to be with her. Then Barri
quit and went back to live with her mother.

Barri went back to Baton Rouge and enrolled again in the
fall, but she only stayed at Southern for one semester before

leaving again. It was, of course, a letdown for me. But I didn't stop trying to get them back into college. I kept on encouraging them to go back to school and get their education. And while Barri never returned to college, Keith has since enrolled at a small college in Illinois and is working toward his degree.

Michael's First Retirement

During the time I was struggling to keep my kids in school, the Bulls were hit with a real bombshell. When I began as the director of community relations in 1992, the Bulls were world champions, and everybody recognized Michael Jordan as the best player in the game, if not the best ever. As expected, he led them to their third straight title during the 1992–93 season, but after the season ended Michael decided to retire and try his hand at pro baseball. That shocked a lot of people, and I think everybody in the organization was disappointed. But while I was surprised when he announced his retirement, I think I understood why he decided to move on to a new challenge.

I first met Michael back in 1989 or 1990, when I was still working at Nordstrom. It was at one of the old-timers games where former players were brought back to play against each other in a preliminary game before the regular NBA game. It was early in his career, but he was already on the verge of breaking the scoring records that I'd held. This was before he became such a big star that he couldn't breathe without someone bugging him for an autograph or following every move he made. When I came out to warm up, he was on the court shooting by himself. I don't think he really knew who I was then, so I walked over and introduced myself. The first thing I noticed was that he was really intense and even seemed a little shy.

We shook hands, and he just said, "It's good to meet you."

"Good to meet you, too," I said.

We only exchanged a few words that day, but afterward I ran into him a few times when I returned to Chicago. By the time he won his third championship ring in 1993, we had developed a pretty good rapport. And when we ran into each other, we'd stop and shoot the breeze. We weren't bosom buddies and we never really socialized a lot, but we had mutual respect. Michael was on his way to becoming an international celebrity. All that media attention forced him to change his lifestyle. There was no way that he could go back to just being one of the guys. After the Bulls won their third title, he couldn't even be seen in public without being surrounded by the press or mobbed by fans. Much of the time he spent away from the basketball court and his family was spent in the company of business associates or other celebrities.

Michael is a special case, of course, since, with the possible exception of Muhammad Ali, no sports star has been as celebrated or admired throughout the world or has benefited as much financially from his athletic skills. Still, as I watched his career escalate, I began to appreciate how truly fortunate today's pro athletes are.

Modern Athletes

Playing any type of professional sport has got to be one of the biggest thrills in life. If you make it to the NBA, you become one of a few hundred guys in the entire world who are able to play at that level. And once you're there, nearly everything is taken care of for you. You get paid extremely well for doing something that you've always enjoyed, and you work only two or three hours a day. Before games, somebody lays out your uniform, and you're pampered by trainers, counselors, and gofers. When you go on the road, someone arranges every step of the trip, packs your bags, and gives you meal money, and you always travel first-class and eat the best food. People look up to you and scramble around trying to get an autograph or just touch you. And people stroke your ego, give you things, or try to enlist you to endorse their products, appear on their TV or radio shows, or just be seen with them. It wasn't quite as extreme when I played, but with all the hype surrounding the game today, I can see why a lot of these young guys are spoiled.

With so many people telling them how great they are, bowing at their feet and worshiping them, it's not surprising that many of the young ballplayers get cocky and walk around with heads as big as their wallets. Back in my day, athletes were heroes, but most guys didn't let it go to their heads. We participated in charity events for free. We took the time to sign autographs for everybody, and we signed them for free. We spoke to everybody. We treated people as people. But nowadays the fans and the media treat young players like gods. We should remember that despite their talent and all the money they're paid, they're just guys who put on basketball uniforms and sneakers, then go out and try to toss a round ball through a hoop. When you really look at it, it's the fans and the media who create many of the sports world's head cases and egomaniacs. We are the ones who exaggerate the importance of playing a simple game, pushed it all out of proportion, and made the guys who play it think they're superhuman.

Down-to-Earth Air

One of the most impressive things about Michael is that he seems to have understood all that from the beginning. He is one of the most competitive people I've ever met, and when he was on the court he had a killer instinct. He absolutely destroyed opponents whenever he could, which is one reason he was so great. But he always seemed to understand that he was playing a game, and he separated that from being a person, a family man and husband, or a friend. With all the acclaim he's received, he still respects the guys who went before him.

Over the years, I've seen a lot of Michael, and I've also met his family. In fact, I know his mother, and she has always impressed me as one of the nicest, classiest people I've ever met. Still, I've never tried to force my way into his life. I never

187

wanted to be one of those guys who hang on to famous people. We know and respect each other, and I've always left it at that. That's one of the reasons we've gotten along so well. I think he respects me for that, and I know that since I arrived in Chicago he's done some pretty good things for me.

After the Bulls won their third consecutive title and Michael repeated as both the league MVP and championship series MVP, I believe he felt that he'd done it all in the NBA. He'd always dreamed of playing major league baseball, and, being a fierce competitor, he was looking for a new challenge. It must have been tough for him to walk away from the NBA when he was at the top of his game and way above anybody else. But I've always felt that it was his determination to follow his own dreams that separated him from the pack and made him such a remarkable athlete. He took his shot at baseball, and when he realized that he couldn't live up to his own standards in that sport, he returned to basketball. And, of course, he led the Chicago Bulls to three more championships from 1996 to 1998.

· During his two-year absence, the Bulls went through a rough period. Scottie Pippen and the rest of the guys gave it all they had, but you can't lose the best player in the game and expect to compete at the same level. And while the team struggled on the court, I was involved in a behind-the-scenes tussle of my own.

Retiring Number 10

Shortly after I arrived in Chicago in 1992, rumors about retiring my jersey had started to circulate. At the time, the only jersey that had been retired by the team was my former teammate Jerry Sloan's number 4. I'd heard the talk, and, of course, I was excited. But I'd also heard that a few people felt that the next number to be retired should be Michael's number 23. Now, Michael was a friend, and I knew that when he finished his career there was no doubt that they'd hang his jersey from the rafters. But I couldn't see why that should keep them from retiring my jersey. Still, there was nothing I could do about it, so I let it go and concentrated on other things.

Then in 1993, the rumors picked up again. It turned out that Reverend Jesse Jackson and some other influential people around town were lobbying to have my number retired. Since I'd gone through it before, I tried not to get too excited. As it turned out, the rumors had some substance this time, and the following year I would receive one of the most prestigious honors an athlete can get.

It all began in the fall of 1993. Reverend Jackson had arranged a sports forum to spotlight the contributions of black athletes at his Operation PUSH headquarters, and I was among those invited. The place was filled with athletes, reporters and sportswriters, TV cameras, and interested spectators. And before the meeting actually began, Reverend Jackson stood up and said, "I have a special announcement to make."

He looked over in my direction and smiled, but I had no idea what he was about to say. Then he turned back to the crowd and said that the owner of the Chicago Bulls, Jerry Reinsdorf, had decided to retire number 10, the jersey of former Bulls All-Star forward Bob Love. Let me tell you, when he said that, all pandemonium broke loose. Everybody in the room stood up and started yelling and clapping, and all the TV cameras swung around and pointed at me. Suddenly I was surrounded by reporters and microphones and flashing cameras. For the first time in years, I was speechless. I just stood there smiling and fighting back the tears.

Then Jerry Reinsdorf got up and made a statement. "Bob Love did a tremendous job for the Chicago Bulls during the time that he was playing," he said, "and now it's our turn to honor him." When he said that, I was so happy I could hardly contain myself. It had all come as a surprise, but at that moment it suddenly seemed as though all the recognition I'd been denied by the team's former owners was being swept away. I felt like I was about to burst with pride. When he finished with his remarks, it must have taken two or three minutes for me to pull myself together and finally say a few words to express my gratitude.

The Other Number 10

The date was set for January, and once the plans had been made the reality began settling in. I was walking around on cloud nine during the next few weeks. But the excitement and the thrill of it didn't come without some disappointment and aggravation. I was upset by some of it, but I got through it. I guess I'd learned to accept those things by then.

A few weeks before the retirement ceremony was scheduled, I got a call from a representative in the Bulls front office. Basically what he said was that they had talked to B. J. Armstrong, the guard who was wearing number 10 at the time, and he resisted changing numbers in the middle of the season. He'd worn the number through a couple of championship years and thought it would be bad luck to switch. It was an awkward situation, because no one wanted to force him to give up the number or embarrass him by ripping the jersey off his back. For awhile, there was even some talk about postponing the date for the ceremony. It got real messy, and finally one of the team representatives suggested that I talk to B. J.

I saw B. J. a day or so later, and he told me that he didn't want to get involved in the affair. He agreed that we should sit down and talk about it, but then he walked off and said, "I really don't want to be put in the middle of all this."

That kind of hurt my feelings, since I knew that if the shoe were on the other foot and I'd have been in his situation, I would have gladly switched my number. I was upset, and I never really discovered what was going through B. J.'s mind, since we never did have that talk. But the whole issue was resolved when Jerry Reinsdorf stepped in and said they were going through with the ceremony. They would hang my jersey alongside Jerry Sloan's, but they also decided to let B. J. wear the jersey as long as he played in Chicago. When he left, they assured me, no one else would wear number 10.

I didn't like it, but I had to accept it.

As it turned out, B. J. only wore the jersey for the remainder of the year. He was released after the 1994 season and signed with Toronto the next year. I have to admit that B. J.'s insisting on wearing the number after it had been retired really tore at me, and during the time he remained with the Bulls things were sometimes tense between us. But on the night of the ceremony, I forgot all about that. I shut out everything but the honor I was about to receive and just enjoyed the moment.

An Emotional Evening

My jersey was retired on January 14, 1994. The Bulls were playing the Utah Jazz at the old Chicago Stadium that night, and the ceremony was held before a jam-packed arena prior to the game. I felt like a little kid out there. It was an emotional evening, one of the most gratifying and exciting moments of my life.

My mom; all of my brothers and sisters; my little boy Nathaniel, who was only six; and most of my children from my first marriage were there. Most of my ex-Bulls teammates showed up. Norm Van Lier, Tom Boerwinkle, my friend Bobby Wilson, and Jerry Sloan were among the players who took part in the ceremony. Even my old high school football coach, William Washington, came in from Louisiana with his wife Dorothy. I couldn't even begin to mention all the friends who were there.

When they gave me the mike to speak that night, I was choked up with emotion and my head was flooded with memories, but they couldn't shut me up. I thanked Coach Washington for helping to keep me on the right path and to achieve as much as I did in high school. I thanked Van Lier and Sloan for the great passes they had made, Boerwinkle for getting all those rebounds and watching my back, and of course I had to thank the Chicago Bulls owner Jerry Reinsdorf for giving me another chance with the team and retiring my jersey.

191

I told my kids how much I appreciate the love and the support they had given me through the good times and the hard times. Finally I got to my mom. She is kind of a shy person, but that night she was so happy and excited for me that she couldn't sit still or hold back her tears. I went over and hugged her. I held her and told her that I loved her and really appreciated all the effort that she put forth in raising me. I thanked her for giving me the strength to face the challenges I'd encountered and for teaching me to never quit. It was a beautiful, moving evening— one I'll never forget.

When I finished, they presented me with a gift that I still treasure. It's a gold ring with a ruby setting and the number 10 inscribed with diamonds. They gave my mother a necklace with a pendant that had the same setting. When she saw it, she just lit up. She was as happy as I'd ever seen her.

After the ceremony ended, we sat together and watched the game. The Bulls were terrific. They routed Utah, 107–91. But my mom and I spent as much time staring up at my jersey as we did watching the action on the court. B. J. wore number 10, but I hardly noticed it that night. I'd just received one of the greatest honors an athlete can receive, and I wasn't about to let anything spoil my evening.

As proud as I was, I knew that my mom was even prouder. She was beaming that evening, and, bless her soul, since then she's had that necklace and pendant around her neck nearly every time I've seen her. My only regret that evening was that my grandmother wasn't there to share the experience with me. Of all the people who had guided and helped me along the way, no one was more supportive than she had been. I missed her more than ever that evening, but I knew that she was watching from heaven and I knew that she was very proud of me.

For a short time, Jerry Sloan's jersey and mine were the only numbers retired by Chicago. Of course, everybody knew that Michael Jordan's jersey would be next. It was just that everyone in the Bulls organization hoped he'd return to the team, and they didn't want to hang up the jersey prematurely. But when Michael began a second year in pro baseball in the spring of 1994, and it seemed that he wouldn't be returning to the Bulls, there was a move to honor his achievements. And on November 1, 1994, there was a spectacular ceremony at the United

Center, the team's newly opened arena, and his number 23 was hung alongside Jerry's and mine.

As it turned out, retiring Michael's jersey was premature. He decided to return to basketball, and about halfway through the 1994–95 season he rejoined the team. Chicago was eliminated early in the play-offs that year, but by the following season it was apparent that Michael had regained his old form. Beginning in 1996, he led the Bulls to three consecutive NBA titles.

Marrying Rachel

Meanwhile, about a year after Michael came out of retirement, I took part in another public ceremony at the United Center— one that was even more personally gratifying than having my number retired.

On December 8, 1995, Rachel and I were married at halftime at center court in the arena. It was the culmination of a three-year courtship that had begun just after I arrived in Chicago, but for Rachel and me it seemed like the start of the happiest time of our lives. Rachel's mother and father came up from Mississippi, and my mother came in from Los Angeles. The Bulls owner and CEO, Jerry Reinsdorf, was my best man, and the Chicago Cubs legend Ernie Banks was in the wedding party. The United Center was jammed that evening, and when we walked out to take our vows, I swear I could feel the affection and warmth swelling up in the crowd. It was an extraordinary, spectacular event.

The Bulls beat the San Antonio Spurs 106–87 that night, and afterward there was a reception for Rachel and me, our friends, all the team members, and the Bulls executives and staff. Everybody had a ball. It was a wonderful way to celebrate our wedding.

We didn't really go on a honeymoon. Instead, we took a few days off to relax and spend some uninterrupted time together. Since then, Rachel and I have brought two wonderful children into the world. The first, Robert Earl Love Jr., was born in July 1995. And in December 1998, we were blessed with a second son, Brodie Alex Benjamin Love. Both of those boys have brightened our lives, and they look like they're going to be great athletes. I can't wait until the time when they start playing ball themselves.

The thrill of being married at center court and sharing the happiness of that evening with thousands of people, of course, will always be among my fondest memories. It was the dramatic beginning of a relationship that has sustained me for years.

Dreams Die Hard

And to this day, when I walk into the United Center I can't help but think about those two special evenings when the Bulls and the Chicago fans honored me. Every time I look up and see my jersey hanging there with the championship banners, with Jerry's and Michael's jerseys, it brings back a rush of memories. I think about the good times, about our team's triumphs and successes, and I'm proud to be associated with the Chicago Bulls organization and honored with players of the stature of Jerry and Michael. But I also remember the hard work—blood, sweat, tears, and trying times—that accompanied those successes. It's rewarding to know that number 10 will always hang in the rafters of the United Center, a tribute to my accomplishments as an athlete. In a way, it symbolizes the fulfillment of a dream that had started in my grandmother's backyard nearly fifty years ago.

But I'd also had another dream as a child in Bastrop. And although its realization never attracted the fanfare that my athletic achievements did, by the time my jersey was retired, I was as much concerned with it as I was with being honored as a basketball player.

17

DREAMS COME TRUE

*If you play the victim, you will always be
one. If you want to succeed, you have to
move on and go for your dream.*

B Y 1994, EIGHT YEARS AFTER I started speech therapy with
Susan Hamilton, I felt as comfortable and assured standing
up to deliver a speech as I had felt going up for a twenty-
foot jump shot or stepping up to the free throw line when I
played basketball. I'd advanced to the point where I could speak
confidently in nearly every situation. It didn't matter whether I
was talking to small groups or large crowds at packed arenas,
to high school students or executives at the most powerful firms
in the country, to avid sports fans or women's groups where
most of the audience didn't know the difference between a
three-point goal and a touchdown. I was as at ease with television appearances as I was with radio interviews. And I had
shared the dais with some of the most popular speakers on the
circuit, ranging from athletic figures like Mike Ditka to politi-
cians and international celebrities like Colin Powell.

I felt that I'd reached the goal that Susan and I had set back
in Seattle. I didn't fool myself into thinking that I'd become the
great orator, the Martin Luther King Jr. I'd dreamed of becoming as a teenager. But I sincerely felt that I had finally become
the effective communicator that I'd set out to be, and I was getting better, becoming more effective every day.

I'd approached that goal when I was at Nordstrom, but as
director of community relations for the Bulls, everything
seemed to fall into place. In Chicago, I had the perfect platform

to describe my experience in sports and my beliefs about facing life's challenges off the playing field.

When I returned to the Bulls in 1992, Jerry Reinsdorf had pulled me aside and assured me that I'd only have to make two or three appearances a day. Then he said, "Look, Bob, you've paid your dues, and you have an inspirational story to tell. All we want you to do is go out and tell that story candidly—the rest will take care of itself."

I couldn't have been happier, and as far as I'm concerned, it is the best job in the world.

"You Should Be Proud of Your father"

I was being paid to go out and honestly express myself and try to help others see that there is no limit to what they can do. I loved it, even though it was sometimes problematic for the people close to me. See, not everyone was thrilled with my talking openly about the hard times that my family and I had gone through, particularly my children. I noticed it most with my youngest daughter, Barri, after I arrived in Chicago. When I appeared at her school and spoke to her classmates, I could tell that she was embarrassed. It was fine when I spoke about my NBA career and the glory days as a player. She was very proud of that. But when I began talking about the struggle to overcome my speech disability and the low points in my life after I left the NBA, she was mortified.

Afterward, I had to sit her down and talk to her privately. "Listen, young lady," I said, "you should be proud of your father. There's no reason to be ashamed of someone with a speech problem or any other disability. You should be proud of my accomplishments, of what I had to go through and what I did to get through it. What's important is that you never heard of me doing anything wrong or getting involved in anything crooked. I didn't let my problems drag me down. I didn't become an alcoholic or resort to drugs or give up on my family."

I told her that I was proud of what I did, proud of having survived some very difficult times and of being able to stand up and relate my story in order to show others that they can do the same thing. "Having a problem is nothing to be ashamed of," I said. "It's throwing in the towel and letting yourself give up that you should worry about. Don't be embarrassed because I'm strong enough, honest enough, to go around telling my story. When I talk about the things I had to face, I'm trying to help other people see how they can overcome their own problems, how they can achieve and be successful no matter how bad things look."

We talked for a long time that evening, and at one point I had to sit back and smile. I realized that I was telling Barri exactly what my grandmother had told me when I'd run home from school to hide out and avoid facing the teasing about my stuttering. I wanted her to understand that no one is perfect, everybody has a handicap, and there is no shame in admitting it. Denying it or trying to hide from it was the real mistake. Not everyone had the same problem that I'd had, but when I stood before them and talked about the hard times and obstacles I'd faced, a lot of people in the audience could relate to it—maybe even leave the auditorium and go on to confront their own demons with a little less fear.

Near the end of our conversation, I told Barri what my grandmother had told me about the importance of hanging on to your dreams and never giving up on yourself. For me, the dream of playing professional basketball had gotten me through the early years of my life, and later, the dream of speaking fluently and effectively had propelled me. "But," I said, "the most important thing is that I never seriously considered giving up and feeling sorry for myself. I'm really happy to be speaking and telling my story. I'm never embarrassed by it, and you shouldn't be embarrassed either."

197

Why I Love to Share My Story

When we finished talking, Barri and I hugged each other, and I think she understood a little more about why speaking was so crucial to me. I know that I felt even stronger about my desire to continue telling my story, sharing the tale of my struggle to overcome a disability and realize a dream. Speaking to people is not just a way of making a living for me; it's an affirmation of the ability that we all share to face an adversary or challenge without fear. And I enjoy it every bit as much as I enjoyed competing in basketball.

I actually get turned on whenever I'm about to stand and speak in front of a crowd. I can feel the excitement building. The adrenaline starts running immediately, and I'm never hesitant or afraid. It's almost like the feeling I had when I stood at midcourt waiting for the tipoff in a big game. In fact, I try to imagine myself waiting for the referee to toss the ball into the air. And every time I stand up to speak, I'm thinking, "It's game time!"

When I start speaking, I try to make people feel good about themselves. That's what I aim for, and when I see an audience responding to the human side of my story, my enthusiasm builds. Helping to create that warmth and affection is an instant rush. It's as if I've broken down some artificial barrier and established contact on an altogether different level. And a lot of times, after I've finished, members of the audience rush up to the stage and greet me as if I were part of their families, as if they had known me forever. It's a wonderful feeling, one that's impossible to describe.

As I've traveled across the country telling my story and trying to get people to draw on their own inner strength and to fight to realize their dreams, I've received as many compliments, as much praise, as I ever received in basketball. While it's seldom publicized and not as dramatic as being chosen to play in an NBA All-Star game or having my jersey retired, it's every bit as rewarding as anything I experienced on the basketball court.

The Greatest Reward

It's those moments at the end of my talks, when members of the audience come up to express their appreciation or relate stories of their own struggles and hardships, that keep me going and make my job so fulfilling. Over the years, there have been hundreds of times when, as a speaker, I've been moved by the audience's reaction. One example was my speech at the Little City Foundation luncheon in Chicago, when, after four or five people broke down and cried, I had to stop and try to compose myself. But those occasions range from the pharmaceutical convention in Dallas, where a representative of the group rushed up and told me that he had never given a speaker a standing ovation before that night; to the Chicago women's group whose members ran up, hugged me, and began shouting, "That was the greatest story we've ever heard!"; or the Boston accountants convention where the chairman pulled me aside and said, "Bob, we're never had anyone come in and talk to us that honestly before. There's not a dry eye in the room. Please, come back and talk to us again next year."

It's those kinds of responses that keep me going, make me love my work.

But the greatest reward is when I realize that I've not only touched people momentarily, but that I've also had some positive impact on their lives. I'll never forget the letter I received from a Notre Dame student who, several months after I spoke to a group from his communications class, wrote me and admitted that he had seriously considered suicide. He was barely getting by in school, his parents had threatened to stop paying his tuition if he didn't improve, and his girlfriend had left him. He was completely down on himself, ready to give up. But after he heard my story, his attitude changed. He wrote that if I could handle what I'd faced, there was no reason that he couldn't deal with his situation. He hadn't overcome all of his problems, but the letter said, "I want you to know that you've given me the courage to go on, stop feeling sorry for myself, and do the best that I can."

Nothing is more gratifying than a letter like that. For one thing, it spotlights the importance of those people who pass through our lives and help us along the way. I know that personally, I've been blessed with friends and family members who have stepped in at just the right time and given me the support or guidance that I've needed. I'll always appreciate and give credit to my mother and grandmother, my high school and college coaches, my children and friends, my speech therapist Susan Hamilton, the owners of Nordstrom, and the present executives and owners of the Chicago Bulls organization, especially Steve Schanwald and Jerry Reinsdorf. Without them, I might have stumbled and never found the courage to pursue my goals. I'm not sure. I am certain that their presence and support made my struggle a lot easier.

I Never Gave Up on My Dreams

But that student's letter also highlights the importance of never letting frustration hold you back. You can't go around carrying a grudge, holding on to negative feelings about someone who might have hurt or misused you. You can't let yourself get caught up in bitterness about the things that have happened to you. If you play the victim, you will always be one. If you want to succeed, you have to move on and go for your dream.

As I point out when I speak, materially, I grew up in the poorest of circumstances. But although I was abused and had a serious disability, there was enough love and caring in my family to keep me on the right track. I reached the top of the athletic world only to fall and hit bottom—alone, penniless, and on welfare. Although I'd been an All-American and All-Pro basketball player, I'd never been totally satisfied. Finally, it was that crash that made me acknowledge the problem that had dogged me since childhood. I began to realize that the inability to communicate was a terrible disability.

But even in the darkest of times, I never gave up or used the awful things that had happened to me as excuses. Instead, I focused on the strength and advice of my grandmother. *If you want something, child, you got to do it for yourself*—I'll never forget those words.

And since God has enabled me to speak, although I can't remember the first or the last basket I made, I can remember almost every speech I've made and thousands of the faces that

I've seen as I've stood at the podium. I'm enjoying myself much more now than I ever did when I was in the NBA.

At this point in my life, I wouldn't trade places with anybody in the world. I never made the kind of money that the current group of NBA stars make, and I don't have the material things that many of them have. What I do have is a genuine concern and respect for the people I meet, and the joy of knowing I've faced the toughest challenge in my life and come out a better person. And it's all because I refused to play the victim. I didn't give up on my dreams.

INDEX

205